First World War
and Army of Occupation
War Diary
France, Belgium and Germany

48 DIVISION
143 Infantry Brigade,
Brigade Machine Gun Company
2 February 1916 - 31 October 1917

WO95/2756/2

The Naval & Military Press Ltd
www.nmarchive.com
Published in association with The National Archives

Published by

The Naval & Military Press Ltd

Unit 10 Ridgewood Industrial Park,

Uckfield, East Sussex,

TN22 5QE England

Tel: +44 (0) 1825 749494

www.naval-military-press.com

www.nmarchive.com

This diary has been reprinted in facsimile from the original. Any imperfections are inevitably reproduced and the quality may fall short of modern type and cartographic standards.

© **Crown Copyright**
Images reproduced by permission of The National Archives, London, England, 2015.

Contents

Document type	Place/Title	Date From	Date To
Heading	WO95/2756/3		
Heading	48th Division 143rd Infy Bde 143rd Machine Gun Coy, Jan 1916-1917 Oct		
Heading	143 Bde M Gun Coy Jan 1916 Vol I		
Miscellaneous	143rd Inf Bde M.G. Company		
War Diary	Chateau La Haie Map 1/40000 Sheet 57d 5.63	02/02/1916	12/02/1916
War Diary	Chateau La Haie	13/02/1916	29/02/1916
Heading	143 Bde M Gun Coy Vol III March 1916		
War Diary	Chateau La Haie France 1/40000 Map Sheet 57d 36b	01/03/1916	09/03/1916
War Diary	Chateau La Haie	10/03/1916	10/03/1916
War Diary	France	11/03/1916	17/03/1916
War Diary	Chateau La Haie	17/03/1916	25/03/1916
War Diary	Fonquevillers	26/03/1916	31/03/1916
Miscellaneous	Machine Gun Coy. 143rd Inf Bde	14/05/1916	14/05/1916
War Diary	Fonquevillers	01/04/1916	16/04/1916
War Diary	Souastre Ref 1/40,000 Map Sheet 57d	01/04/1916	26/04/1916
War Diary	Souastre	27/04/1916	30/04/1916
Miscellaneous	To D.A.G 3rd Echelon	03/06/1916	03/06/1916
War Diary	Fonquevillers	01/05/1916	05/05/1916
War Diary	Fonquevillers & Souastre	06/05/1916	06/05/1916
War Diary	Couin	07/05/1916	14/05/1916
War Diary	Bretel Ref Map 1/40,000 Sheet 57 D	15/05/1916	25/05/1916
War Diary	Couin Authie	26/05/1916	27/05/1916
War Diary	Bretel	28/05/1916	31/05/1916
Miscellaneous	Machine Gun Coy 143rd Inf Bde	10/07/1916	10/07/1916
War Diary	Couin	01/06/1916	01/06/1916
War Diary	Hebuterne & Sailly Map France 57 D NE 1/20,000	02/06/1916	30/06/1916
Heading	143rd Inf. Bde 48th Div. War Diary 143rd Machine Gun Company July 1916		
Heading	War Diary Of 143rd Machine Gun Company From 1st July 1916 To 31st July 1916 Vol VII		
War Diary	Hebuterne	01/07/1916	04/07/1916
War Diary	Couin	05/07/1916	12/07/1916
War Diary	Bouzincourt	13/07/1916	15/07/1916
War Diary	Albert	13/07/1916	26/07/1916
War Diary	Bouzincourt	27/07/1916	31/07/1916
Heading	143rd Brigade 48th Division 143rd Brigade Machine Gun Company August 1916		
War Diary	Coulonvillers Ref Map Lens II 1/100,000 5 A	01/08/1916	08/08/1916
War Diary	Gezaincourt	09/08/1916	09/08/1916
War Diary	Lealvillers Ref Map Lens II 1/100000 6.G	10/08/1916	13/08/1916
War Diary	Bouzaincourt	14/08/1916	15/08/1916
War Diary	Map Ovillers 57d. S.E 4 1/10000	16/08/1916	17/08/1916
War Diary	Map Ovillers 1/5000	18/08/1916	27/08/1916
War Diary	Ref Map 57 D S.E 1/2000	28/08/1916	31/08/1916
War Diary	Lens II Map	28/08/1916	31/08/1916
Heading	48th Division 143rd Infantry Bde. 143rd Machine Gun Company September 1916		
Heading	War Diary 143rd Machine Gun Co 1st September 1916 To 30th September 1916 Volume 9		

War Diary	Authie Lens II F5	01/09/1916	10/09/1916
War Diary	Bretel Lens II Map D5	11/09/1916	17/09/1916
War Diary	Prouville Lens II B5	18/09/1916	23/09/1916
War Diary	Grimont Lens II 4/5 B	23/09/1916	23/09/1916
War Diary	Heuzecourt Lens II Map	24/09/1916	24/09/1916
War Diary	Ref Map 1/100,000 Lens II Grimont 4/5 B	25/09/1916	25/09/1916
War Diary	Bernaville 5/B	26/09/1916	26/09/1916
War Diary	Grimont	27/09/1916	28/09/1916
War Diary	Grenas 5/F	29/09/1916	29/09/1916
War Diary	Souastre 5/G	30/09/1916	30/09/1916
Heading	War Diary 143rd MG Co. From 1st Oct To-31st Oct		
War Diary	Souastre Map (D22) 57D N.E Ed.2b 1/20000	01/10/1916	01/10/1916
War Diary	Hebuterne	02/10/1916	05/10/1916
War Diary	Hebuterne	05/10/1916	05/10/1916
War Diary	St Amand D9-10	05/10/1916	08/10/1916
War Diary	St Amand Trance	09/10/1916	18/10/1916
War Diary	St Amand	19/10/1916	20/10/1916
War Diary	Grand Rullencourt	21/10/1916	26/10/1916
War Diary	Becourt	27/10/1916	31/10/1916
Heading	War Diary 143 Machine Gun Coy November 1st-November 30th 1916		
War Diary	Albert	01/11/1916	02/11/1916
War Diary	Fricourt	03/11/1916	10/11/1916
War Diary	Martinpuich	11/11/1916	15/11/1916
War Diary	Contalmaison	16/11/1916	23/11/1916
War Diary	Martinpuich	24/11/1916	30/11/1916
Heading	War Diary 143rd Machine Gun Coy From Dec 1st 1916 To Dec 31st 1916 Vol 12		
War Diary	Martinpuich	01/12/1916	02/12/1916
War Diary	Contalmaison	03/12/1916	08/12/1916
War Diary	Martinpuich	09/12/1916	10/12/1916
War Diary	Contalmaison	11/12/1916	15/12/1916
War Diary	Millencourt	16/12/1916	28/12/1916
War Diary	Warloy	29/12/1916	31/12/1916
Heading	War Diary 143 Machine Gun Coy January 1st To January 31st 1917 Vol 13		
War Diary	Warloy	01/01/1917	09/01/1917
War Diary	Bettincourt	10/01/1917	27/01/1917
War Diary	Mericourt	28/01/1917	31/01/1917
Heading	War Diary 143 Machine Gun Coy Feb 1st 1917-Feb 28/16 Vol 14		
War Diary		01/02/1917	31/03/1917
Heading	War Diary 143rd Machine Gun Coy 1st April-30 April 1917 Vol 16		
War Diary		01/04/1917	30/04/1917
Heading	War Diary 143rd Machine Gun Company 1st May 1917 To 31st May 1917 Vol 17		
War Diary		01/05/1917	31/05/1917
Heading	War Diary 143rd Machine Gun Coy 1st June 1917-30th June		
War Diary	In The Field	01/06/1917	30/06/1917
Heading	War Diary 143rd Machine Gun Coy 1st July 1917-31st July 1917 Vol 19		
War Diary	Gommiecourt	01/07/1917	03/07/1917
War Diary	Bienvillers	04/07/1917	31/07/1917
Heading	War Diary 143 M.G. Coy 1st Aug 1917-31 Aug 1917		

War Diary	In The Field	01/08/1917	31/08/1917
Heading	War Diary 143 Machine Gun Coy 1st Sept 1917-30th Sept 1917 Vol 21		
War Diary	In The Field	01/09/1917	30/09/1917
Heading	War Diary 143rd Machine Gun Company 1st Oct 1917 31st Oct 1917 Vol 22		
War Diary	Dambre Camp Vlamertinge	01/10/1917	03/10/1917
War Diary	In The Line	04/10/1917	04/10/1917
War Diary	St Julien	05/10/1917	08/10/1917
War Diary	Poperinghe	09/10/1917	13/10/1917
War Diary	Mont St Eloi	14/10/1917	14/10/1917
War Diary	Vimy	15/10/1917	31/10/1917

n00518256/3

48TH DIVISION
143RD INFY BDE

143RD MACHINE GUN COY.

JAN 1916-~~FEB 1918~~

1917 OCT

TO ITALY

48/5
1 & 3 Bde to Gun Coy
Jan 1916.
V & I

Jan '16
Feb '16

1916   143rd Infy Bde
       M.G. Company

Jan 8.   M.G Company formed in
         143rd Infy Bde. Battalions
         take over 4 Lewis guns
         each. M.G Company takes
         over 12 Vickers & 4 Maxims.

9   Bishop of Birmingham
         visited the Bde & held service
         in the School of Instruction
         at BAYENCOURT.

10.   Disposition of M G's in front
         line adjusted in consequence
         of extra Lewis Guns.

11   Nothing of interest to report

12   do   do

13   Sections relieved. New
         dispositions of guns
         complete. Guns in reserve
         at LA HAIE & BAYENCOURT
         Teams at BAYENCOURT undergoing
         systematic training.

14.   Work started of M.G positions

in Brigade line.

15. Commencement of horse standings at BAYENCOURT. Inspection of Transport by O/C M.G. Company.

16. Our M.G's cooperated with 143 Bde Trench Mortars on Enemy trenches opposite M Sector

17. 20 allied aeroplanes passed over LA HAIE at about 11.30am

18. Enemy's wiring parties were disturbed by M.G. fire last night.

19. Enemy fired new caustic shells heavily into M Sector. Our M.G's fired at suspected places without result.

20. Handed 4 Maxim Guns to 49th Division. Received in Exchange 4 Vickers Guns.

21. Enemy trench mortars active again. All shots into M Sector.

22. Our artillery bombarded Enemy trenches south of GOMMECOURT WOOD.

23. Nothing to report

24. Enemy fired several canister bombs into M Sector during the early hours of the morning.

25. Intense bombardment of M Sector from 2 am - 2.30 am with Minenwerfer, Howitzers & Field Guns. Our M.G North of Gommecourt Road fired over 1000 rounds towards GOMMECOURT & the GOMMECOURT - FONQUEVILLERS Road. No result observed. Enemy party afterwards found to have entered our trenches. None were seen by our sentries.

26. Quiet day. Nothing of interest to report.

27. 4 New emplacements made in L Sector for the purpose of supporting a raid proposed for the night of 29.30.
7.15 pm. Gas alarm was received (Wind due West). Company stood to in Smoke Helmets for 1 hour. Report then contradicted.

28. 7am another false gas alarm was received. Guns laid & sighted on points in enemy line opposite L Sector.

29. Raid on enemy trenches was postponed as night was dark & foggy.

30.31. Nothing to Report

WAR DIARY or INTELLIGENCE SUMMARY

Army Form C. 2118

143 M.G. Coy

Feb 1916

Place	Date	Hour	Summary of Events and Information	Remarks and references to Appendices
CHATEAU DE LA HAIE	Feb 1916 1.		Enemy patrol seen in our wire opposite M Section. Lt was driven off by rifle & M.G. fire. Our artillery bombarded enemy trenches north of GOMMECOURT.	over
	2.		Quiet day.	over
Mont St Eloi	3.		Enemy artillery active.	"
Sheet 57D S.6.G.3	4.		Capt Lees taken over our duties. Our artillery carried out bombardment of enemy trenches south of PARC de GOMMECOURT. Enemy retired by heavy shelling of our Sections at FONQUEVILLERS almost & men wounded	"
	5.		Capt Sutton 1. S.L.I. Egft. to take up appointment as D.A.A. & Q.M.G. 57th Div. Capt Ellison took up duties of a S.I. B.M.	"
	6) 7) 8)		Nothing to report	"
	9) 10)		Enemy artillery active. They appear to be registering all points behind our front line with 4.2" shells. Yt. seems that there is great artillery activity. This fact	"
	11		Enemy shelled HEBUTERNE fairly heavily about 70cm	"
	12		Nothing to report	"

WAR DIARY or INTELLIGENCE SUMMARY

Army Form C. 2118

Place	Date	Hour	Summary of Events and Information	Remarks and references to Appendices
CHATEAU LA HAIE.	13ᵗʰ		At midnight our guns fired 200 rounds on enemy front & second line trenches. Enemy retaliation was feeble.	copy
	14.		Nothing to report	-
	15.		L section extended of include trenches 13.14.15. TM section extended to SD.51.52. Ishler over gun from 7ᵗʰ (Worcesters) 143 Bde. Take over the whole of FONCQUEVILLERS.	-
	16/17		Nothing to report.	-
	18.		Enemy bombarded M section heavily from 1.30 am - 2.30 am. Much damage done to our trenches. Casualties 6. Enemy made raid on 12ᵗʰ Bde.	-
	19			-
	20.		Our artillery shelled GOMMECOURT trenches at 10.30 p.m. Enemy reply was feeble.	-
	21		Enemy bombarded. Then artillery apparently registering through night of L Section.	-
	22.		Weather very cold. Sergt. Free D. Brown	-
	23 24		Nothing to report	-

Army Form C. 2118

WAR DIARY
or
INTELLIGENCE SUMMARY
(Erase heading not required.)

Instructions regarding War Diaries and Intelligence Summaries are contained in F. S. Regs., Part II. and the Staff Manual respectively. Title Pages will be prepared in manuscript.

Place	Date	Hour	Summary of Events and Information	Remarks and references to Appendices
CHATEAU LA HAIE	25		Very cold day. Snowing hard. Raining very hard.	
	26		Nothing of interest.	
	27		Heavy thaw. Trenches very wet & muddy. Green.	
	28		Trenches 53-57 inclusive were taken over from 144 Bde.	
	29		New distribution 1-18 A section 19-57 M Section ?	

Andrew Jn Capt
Comdg 143 Bde. M.G.Coy.

1875 Wt. W 393/826 1,000,000 4/15 J.B.C. & A. A.D.S.S./Forms/C. 2118.

48

143 Bde M Gun Coy
Vol III

March 1916.

Army Form C. 2118

WAR DIARY
or
INTELLIGENCE SUMMARY
(Erase heading not required.)

143rd Bde MACHINE GUN COY

Place	Date	Hour	Summary of Events and Information	Remarks and references to Appendices
CHATEAU LA HAIE FRANCE Hubert not Sheet 57D S.6.b	1/3/16		Enemy fired 16 Canister Bombs in the neighbourhood of the GOMMECOURT ROAD. 6 of them failed to explode.	
	2		All henceforth, Section D not a 2 Companies of the Batt at BAYENCOURT move to SOUASTRE.	
	3		Nothing to report.	
	4		Very Heavy snow	
	5		Slight thaw. Trenches in very bad state.	
	6		Nothing to report.	
	7		Orders received from 48th Div. to gun up trenches 50-57 & 112 Infy Bde on front.	
	8		Trenches handed over to 37th Div. (8th East Lancs 112 Infy Bde). Our line now trenches 1-23.	
	9		Attended conference of B.G.C. CO's &c with reference to being ready to attack at short notice.	

Army Form C. 2118

WAR DIARY
or
INTELLIGENCE SUMMARY
(Erase heading not required.)

Instructions regarding War Diaries and Intelligence Summaries are contained in F.S. Regs., Part II. and the Staff Manual respectively. Title Pages will be prepared in manuscript.

Place	Date	Hour	Summary of Events and Information	Remarks and references to Appendices
CHATEAU LA HAIE FRANCE	1916 March 10		Nothing to report.	
	11		Six Stokens mountings in rest. Have along southern line.	
	12		Nothing to report.	
	13		R.E. have fitted up a shelter for sentry shelter bracket into the parapet. This completes the bracket to the front.	
	14		Demonstration by Grenade School of a Grenade attack, demolition of wire by Bangalore Torpedo & Walts Fused stormy etc. Very warm & sunny	
	15			
	16		Conference with officers & certain rank & commanders on the German known attacks	
	17		Several M.G. emplacements built & suffered rase	

WAR DIARY
or
INTELLIGENCE SUMMARY

Army Form C. 2118

(Erase heading not required.)

Place	Date	Hour	Summary of Events and Information	Remarks and references to Appendices
CHATEAU LA HAIE	17"		Major WHALLEY on leave. Thanks to Bde Major.	
	18	5 p.m.	Conference at Brigade Headquarters with reference to Raid on enemy trenches. Details completed.	J.A.
		10 p.m.	Field Guns bombarded enemy trenches in preparation for raid. Enemy retaliated with 4.2" + 5.9" shells on FONQUEVILLERS.	
	19	2 A.M.	Enemy opened heavy bombardment all along our line and made raid on trenches of Brigade on our right. This was unsuccessful. All battalions "stood to". "Stand down" went at 3. A.M. Building emplacements for disappearing mountings on front line trenches of this brigade.	J.A.
	20.		Fine day bright sunshine. Building gun emplacements in preparation for our raid on enemy trenches. Our guns bombarded enemy trenches at 11 P.M.	J.A.
	21.		Enemy quiet. Preparations for raid.	J.A.
	22	9 p.m.	Our guns bombarded enemy trenches. Preparations for raid. Brought up 6 guns from reserve. Laid these at dusk. 12 M.N. Gunners stood by guns ready for raid	J.A.
	23	12 m. 1.14 a.m.	Our guns bombarded enemy front line trenches for 6 minutes. Machine guns co-operating. Guns lifted. raiding party of 8th Warwicks entered enemy trenches. Captured one prisoner. Smoke helmets and got useful information. Raid very successful. Party from 5th Warwicks found more wire than was anticipated and were discovered by enemy before they got through. One man of M.G. Coy wounded. Machine guns kept up fire all the time under fairly heavy bombardment.	J.A.
	23.	2 A.M.	Enemy bombarded our trenches are FONQUEVILLERS for ½ hour.	J.A.
	24		Relief day A+C sections came out B+D sections went into trenches	J.A.
	25.		Increased Machine Gun + Rifle fire from enemy trenches. No shelling.	J.A.

Army Form C. 2118

WAR DIARY
or
INTELLIGENCE SUMMARY

(Erase heading not required.)

Instructions regarding War Diaries and Intelligence Summaries are contained in F.S. Regs., Part II. and the Staff Manual respectively. Title Pages will be prepared in manuscript.

Place	Date	Hour	Summary of Events and Information	Remarks and references to Appendices
FONQUEVILLERS	26/3/16		Enemy artillery quiet. Enemy machine guns active.	J.H.
Do.	27		Bright sunshine. Lt Howat attended conference with O.C. 1/8 R. Wark. Regt. dispositions in case of attack.	J.H.
Do.	28		Very quiet day. Nothing to report.	J.H.
Do.	29		Snow fell heavily most of day. Enemy artillery quiet. Enemy machine guns active on FONQUEVILLERS.	J.H.
Do.	30		Enemy 7 and 9 inch MINENWERFEN again in action. These have been quiet for some time.	J.H.
Do.	31	6pm -9pm	Received official intimation that this division (48th) is now in VIII Corps. Considerable activity of enemy minenwerfer on trenches of left sector of this brigade.	J.H.

John Howat Lieut for Capt
Machine Gun Coy
143rd Infantry Brigade.

Machine Gun Coy. 143rd S. Bde.   48

M.G. 86.

To
D.A.G.   14/5/16
3rd Echelon.

Attached please find War Diary for
April 1916, relating to 143rd S. Bde. Machine
Gun Coy.

Vol 4

John Howarth Fox Capt.
Cmdg. 143rd Bde. M. G. Coy.

Army Form C. 2118

WAR DIARY
or
INTELLIGENCE SUMMARY
(Erase heading not required.)

April 1916

Place	Date	Hour	Summary of Events and Information	Remarks and references to Appendices
FONQUEVILL ERS + SOUASTRE	1/4/16		~~Nothing to report~~ Left section Heavily shelled.	J.H.
Ref: 1/40,000 Sh 2	2		Nothing to report.	J.H.
Sheet 57 D.	3		ditto ditto.	J.H.
	4		ditto ditto Shrapnel Helmets issued to this Coy.	J.H.
	5		Horses moved out of stables to open standings. Fine day Bright sunshine	J.H.
	6		Nil.	J.H.
	7		Received reinforcement of 2 men from MACHINE GUN CORPS Base Depot. Fine day bright sunshine.	J.H.
	8		Received 4 men from 15, 16, 17 & 18 R. Warks. to be attached to transport. 1 man returns from leave.	J.H.
	9		Received one remount. Sections relieved in line	J.H.
	10		Lieuts: Howat & Arend attend one days course of instruction at 48th Division Anti-Gas School. Lieut. O'Donnell & Pte. Smith R.J. attend 14 days Vickers Course at Machine Gun School CAMIERS.	J.H.
	11		Lieut Poynting + 2 O.R. proceed on leave.	J.H.
	12		Bright Sunshine. Very warm. Lieut Howat assumes Command of Coy.	J.H.
	13		All officers and men on leave recalled. Leave London 16th inst. 1 Bankers-permen withdrawn & returned Ordnance	J.H.
	14		1 O.R. returns from leave.	J.H.
	15		Nothing to report.	J.H.
	16		Capt Ellington (O.C. Coy) returns from leave & takes over Command of Coy.	J.H.

Army Form C. 2118

WAR DIARY
or
INTELLIGENCE SUMMARY

(Erase heading not required.)

Instructions regarding War Diaries and Intelligence Summaries are contained in F.S. Regs., Part II. and the Staff Manual respectively. Title Pages will be prepared in manuscript.

Place	Date	Hour	Summary of Events and Information	Remarks and references to Appendices
BOUQSTRE. Ref 1/40,000 map Sheet 57.D.	17/4/16		Sections relieve.	J.H.
	18.		Weather breaks down. Horses taken off open standings & put into stables. I.O.R. returns from leave. Pte Horris comes out of trenches for instruction in interior economy prior to taking Commission.	J.H.
	19.		1.O.R. returns from leave. 2/Lt STYNTON F.C.P. joins Coy as reinforcement from Machine gun Corps base.	J.H.
	20.		Received draft of 5 mules to replace complete establishment	J.H.
	21.		Sgt Bennett of this Coy. instructs 144 & 74 Bde M.G. Coy in Vickers gun.	J.H.
	22.		Nothing to report.	J.H.
	23.		Lieut. Docker P. returns from 5 weeks special leave. C.Q.M. Sgt Brown & Pte Harrison proceed on one months leave on re-engagement.	J.H.
	24.		Pte Marshall. 5. died of wounds received to day.	J.H.
	25.		Lt. Arend & I.O.R. proceed on leave to England.	J.H.
	26.		88 Sgt Daykin killed in action. This Coy. relieved by 144 & Bde M.G. by in front line trenches	J.H.
BOUQSTRE.	27.		Lt O'DONNELL & Pte SMITH K.J. return from M.G. Course at CAMIERS	J.H.
	28.		Nothing to report.	J.H.
	29.		4 Officers & 1 N.C.O attended FLAMENWERFER demonstration	J.H.
	30.		2 NCO's proceed to CAMIERS for 14 days VICKERS GUN COURSE	J.H.

Answering to C/O MG Coy
Draft 143 Bde MG Coy

To | D.A.G.
3rd Echelon.

    Enclosed herewith please find War Diary (Original) for May 1916. of 143rd Bde Machine Gun Company.

3/6/16.

                John Howatt Lieut.
                143rd Bde M.G. Coy.

143rd Bde. M.G. Coy 48

WAR DIARY or INTELLIGENCE SUMMARY

Army Form C. 2118

(Erase heading not required.)

Instructions regarding War Diaries and Intelligence Summaries are contained in F.S. Regs., Part II. and the Staff Manual respectively. Title Pages will be prepared in manuscript.

Place	Date	Hour	Summary of Events and Information	Remarks and references to Appendices
FONQUEVILLERS	1/5/16	2 P.M. 11. P.M.	One section took over emplacements in front line from 144TH BDE M.G.Coy. One occupied positions in FONQUEVILLERS	J.H.
Do	2		Left sector heavily bombed with MINENWERFER.	J.H.
Do	3		Intermittent shelling throughout the day.	J.H.
Do	4	2.30 P.M	Heavy bombardment on our left near MONCHY-AU-BOIS. Officers of 137TH BDE M.G. Coy came up to reconnoitre our line prior to relieving this Coy.	J.H.
Do	5		Officers 137TH BDE M.G. Coy again reconnoitring line. 143RD INF. BDE relieved by 137TH INF. BDE in trenches at FONQUEVILLERS.	J.H.
FONQUEVILLERS to SOUASTRE	6	8 A.M.	137TH Bde M.G. Coy relieved this Coy. 143RD Bde M.G.Coy moved into Camp at COUIN	J.H.
COUIN	7		Three left for base for discharge (time expired) Church parade + inspection by G.O.C. 48th Division 1 Reinforcement arrived from M.G.C. Base Depot	J.H.
	8		Showery day. Routine Work. LT. BISSEKER + 2 new offrs proceed on leave.	J.H.
	9		Very wet day. Pte Morris of this Coy. Commissioned + posted to Coy.	J.H.
	10		LT BUCK proceeded to BRETEL to arrange billets for Coy. Received orders to move to BRETEL at 5 A.M. tomorrow morning	J.H.
	11		Left COUIN 5 A.M. + marched to BRETEL. arrived there 10 A.M.	J.H.
	12		Nothing to report.	J.H.
	13		Lieut Stanton went sick to hospital. G.O.C. 48th Division inspected this Coy. Very wet day.	J.H.
	14		Church Parade. Day fair but cloudy.	J.H.

Army Form C. 2118

WAR DIARY
or
INTELLIGENCE SUMMARY
(Erase heading not required.)

Instructions regarding War Diaries and Intelligence Summaries are contained in F. S. Regs., Part II. and the Staff Manual respectively. Title Pages will be prepared in manuscript.

Place	Date	Hour	Summary of Events and Information	Remarks and references to Appendices
BRETEL. Ref. map. 1/40,000 Sheet 57.D.	15		Unpleasant day. Coy bathed. Rain hampered training. Lectures held in billets.	Q.
	16		Fine day, bright sunshine, warm. Coy training 7 A.M – 12.30 p.m.	J.H.
	17.		Fine day. Coy training. Shooting on range.	Ama.
	18		2/Lieut STANTON returned from hospital.	Ama.
	19		Nothing to report. ~~Returning to usual~~ 143rd BRIGADE Route March.	Ama.
	20.		Bright sun. Routine training.	Ama.
	21		143rd BRIGADE Church Parade. Company sports in afternoon: Lieut HOWATT + 2 men proceed on leave.	Ama.
	22		2/Lieut NORRIS returns from leave and takes on Strength of Company.	Ama.
	23		LIEUT BISSEKER goes to hospital: Usual training 7am – 12.30 pm.	Ama.
	24		Long rifles withdrawn and number of men inoculated – 8 Reinforcements arrive from M.G.C. base depot	Ama.
	25		New short rifles issued. Shooting on range.	Ama.
	26		Company leave billets at 2.30 a.m. to proceed to COUIN. Breakfast en route.	Ama.
COUIN AUTHIE			Paraded Ham to proceed on BRIGADE Scheme – between COIGNEUX and COUIN. Returning to huts at COUIN at 10.30 a.m. Paraded again at 5.30 p.m. to continue Tactical Exercise, finishing at AUTHIE where the Company were in huts at 10 p.m. It was found during the Exercise that although no heavy tripods were carried for the guns, thirty carrying one man. it was impossible owing to small establishment to keep up a satisfactory	

1875 Wt. W593/826 1,000,000 4/15 J.B.C. & A. A.D.S.S./Forms/C. 2118.

Army Form C. 2118

WAR DIARY
or
INTELLIGENCE SUMMARY
(Erase heading not required.)

Instructions regarding War Diaries and Intelligence Summaries are contained in F.S. Regs., Part II. and the Staff Manual respectively. Title Pages will be prepared in manuscript.

Place	Date	Hour	Summary of Events and Information	Remarks and references to Appendices
COUIN	26		Supply of ammunition and boxes of belts. LIEUT O'DONNELL returns from leave.	Ptd.
AUTHIE	27		Parade at AUTHIE at 6.30 am. to proceed back to BRETEL. arriving at billets there at 10.15 am.	Ptd.
BRETEL	28	9 am.	BRIGADE Church Parade.	Ptd.
	29.		Usual company training. Shooting practice on Range with Vickers Guns.	Ptd.
	30.		Inspection of guns. Limbers Kit &c. preparatory to moving up to Trenches. LIEUT BUCK goes on leave.	Ptd.
	31	4.30 am	Parade at BRETEL at 4.30 am and move to COUIN. Breakfasting en route. Arrive at COUIN at 10.15 am.	Ptd.

John Howarth Lieut for Capt
Comdg 143rd Bde. Machine Gun Coy.

M.G. 1/73

Machine Gun Coy. 143rd Inf Bde.

2/
D.A.G.
3rd Echelon.

Herewith "Original" War Diary, of above named Unit, for month of June. [1916]

10/7/16.

Ralph W. Ainsworth Lt.
Cmdg. 143rd Bde. M. G. Coy.

143rd Bde. MACHINE GUN COMPANY. 48

Army Form C. 2118

WAR DIARY or INTELLIGENCE SUMMARY

JUNE 1-30

Vol 6

(Erase heading not required.)

Place	Date	Hour	Summary of Events and Information	Remarks and references to Appendices
COUIN	1/6/16	9 P.M	Left COUIN for trenches at HEBUTERNE. 1/2 Coy relieved 144 Bde MG Coy in trenches. 1/2 Coy in billets at SAILLY-AU-BOIS.	J.H.
HEBUTERNE SAILLY.	2nd		Wind not favourable for gas attack on part of enemy. Intermittent shelling through out the day.	J.H.
MAP FRANCE 57 D.N.E. 1/20,000.	3rd		Wind West. 15 miles per hour. Small bombing attacks between battalions on our left and enemy between 9pm + 10pm	J.H.
	4th		Midnight 3/4th. We opened heavy bombardment on enemy trenches. Two divisions on our right carried out raid on enemy's trenches. Bombardment ceased at 1-40 am. Men in SAILLY-AU-BOIS mounted dugouts pursuant the expected retaliation on part of enemy. This did not come off.	J.H.
	5th		Wind West 15.20 miles/hour. Showery weather. 1 NCO + man proceeded on one month's leave on reengagement. 2 Sections from SAILLY on working parties building gun emplacements in front line trenches.	J.H.
	6th		Very wet day. 2 Sections at SAILLY on working parties in front line trenches support trenches on gun emplacements. Enemy quiet practically no shelling. Gun specially laid to cover working parties on both flanks.	J.H.
	7th		Wet morning. A+C Sections relieved B+D sections in trenches.	J.H.
	8th	10pm 7pm	Some MINENWERFER activity about 10 pm. otherwise quiet night. About 100 shells fired into HEBUTERNE	J.H.
	9th		Considerable artillery activity on both sides during night 8/9th. Very wet all day.	J.H.
	10th	12M 11.P.M.	Very wet day. Heavy bombardment on our front line. Brigade on our left.	J.H.

Army Form C. 2118

WAR DIARY
or
INTELLIGENCE SUMMARY
(Erase heading not required.)

Instructions regarding War Diaries and Intelligence Summaries are contained in F.S. Regs., Part II. and the Staff Manual respectively. Title Pages will be prepared in manuscript.

Place	Date	Hour	Summary of Events and Information	Remarks and references to Appendices
HEBUTERNE & SAILLY	11/6/16	10.30 AM	German heavy shells on edge of HEBUTERNE. Day fair but cloudy, inclined to rain.	J.H.
MAP France 57D.N.E. 1/20,000	12.		143 Bde M.G. Coy relieved by M.G. Coy of 145 Bde.	Cur 2
	13th to 21st		M.G. company at COUIN engaged in training. Officers & 16 men are now attached from the Battalions to assist in company work on the etc. The small establishment of the M.G. Company makes this addition imperative.	/
	22.		M.G. company relieved the 145 Bde M.G. Coy having put in 12 guns in the line. The remainder in SAILLY. Guns held in reserve in SAILLY.	/
	23		Very violent bombardment making trenches in very bad state.	/
	24.		Our front started bombardment at 7 am shelled intermittently all day. Machine guns all laid on enemy front line.	/
	25.		Bombard ment continued. Our MG's left ammunition & emits & communication trenches shewed up well found in fath in rain. Expenditure of SAA for 24 hours was 10,000.	/

WAR DIARY
or
INTELLIGENCE SUMMARY
(Erase heading not required.)

Army Form C. 2118

Instructions regarding War Diaries and Intelligence Summaries are contained in F.S. Regs., Part II. and the Staff Manual respectively. Title Pages will be prepared in manuscript.

Place	Date	Hour	Summary of Events and Information	Remarks and references to Appendices
	26th		Intense bombardment. M.G's fire replied to even the most of our guns being discharged. The Jews were strewn full a hundred strong artillery retaliation.	
	27/28		Bombardment continued.	
	29		Should have been two days of assault. This was put forward given all prepared for coming the assault.	
	30		3,1,5, s6 Run tomorrow. Most of our bottom on the forward slop of the hill a few good after trenches for bayonet command first of them.	

Signed (illegible) Lt for
Cmdg. 143rd Bde. M. G. Coy.

143rd Inf.Bde.
48th Div.

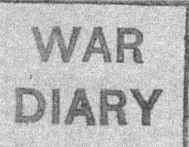

143rd MACHINE GUN COMPANY.

J U L Y

1 9 1 6

143rd Inf.Bde.
48th Div.

CONFIDENTIAL.

WAR DIARY OF

143rd Machine Gun Company.

From 1st July, 1916 to 31st July, 1916.

Vol. VII.

INTELLIGENCE SUMMARY

(Erase heading not required.)

Instructions regarding War Diaries and Intelligence Summaries are contained in F. S. Regs., Part II. and the Staff Manual respectively. Title Pages will be prepared in manuscript.

Place	Date	Hour	Summary of Events and Information	Remarks and references to Appendices
HEBUTERNE	1/7/16		6.30 a.m. Intense bombardment of enemy lines from SERRE to GOMMECOURT. Gave overhead supporting fire to 31st Division attacking SERRE. 1st LT HOWATT wounded. 31st Div. back to original British lines by night fall.	Appx. a.
	2/7/16		Quiet day, nothing to report.	Appx. a.
	3/7/16		Stand to in evening. Every gun sent up to trenches – night fairly quiet.	Appx. a.
	4/7/16		Relieved by 145th M.G. Coy. about 6 p.m. Moved to billets in COUIN. Very wet. 2/LT PATTERSON joins Company	Appx. a.
COUIN	5/7/16		Inspected by Gen. Sir Aylmer Hunter Weston. Cleaned guns and equipment.	Appx. a.
	6/7/16		Moved from billets in Divisional School. COUIN to bivouacs near COUIN.	Appx. a.
	7/7/16		Very wet. No work done.	Appx. a.
	8/7/16		Cleaning and general training. 2 p.m. Received orders that we were now in Corps Reserve.	Appx. a.
	9/7/16		Working party clearing trenches near LA SIGNY FARM. 2.30 p.m. to 10.30 p.m. Attached men trained in gun drill	Appx. a.
	10/7/16		Tested guns and training	Appx. a.
	11/7/16	7 a.m.	Working party repairing roads at COIGNEUX under 13.E. Balance of Company training.	Appx. a.
	12/7/16	7 a.m.	Working party as on 11th.	Appx. a.
BOUZINCOURT – ALBERT	13/7/16	1 p.m.	Moved from COUIN by motor lorries to BOUZINCOURT. Later moved to dug-outs in LA BOISELLE – shelled on way up. A Section moved up to front line to support attack in morning.	Appx. a.
	14/7/16		Attack failed and guns had to be withdrawn. LT STANTON wounded – guns practically useless with dirt and mud.	Appx. a.
	15/7/16		Two guns sent to support patrols of 4th Rl. Main R. Patrols could not leave trenches owing to enemy M.G. fire.	Appx. a.

INTELLIGENCE SUMMARY

(Erase heading not required.)

Instructions regarding War Diaries and Summaries are contained in F.S. Regs., Part II. and the Staff Manual respectively. Title Pages will be prepared in manuscript.

Place	Date	Hour	Summary of Events and Information	Remarks and references to Appendices
ALBERT	16/7/16		Two M.G's sent out to support 1/5th R.War.R in attack on trench N of OVILLERS. Batt got objective without trouble but thanks in air. Guns could not be sent over.	Appx.
	17/7/16		Two guns sent up to OVILLERS which 1/6th R.War.R. had consolidated.	Appx. Appx.
	18/7/16		New dispositions of guns for narrow front not proceeded with owing to 145th M.G. Coy relieving in trenches.	Appx.
	19/7/16		Relieved by 145th M.G. Coy. and moved back to billets in BOUZINCOURT.	Appx.
	20/7/16		Guns and material cleaned.	Appx.
	21/7/16		Gun drill and overhaul of equipment.	Appx.
	22/7/16	6.30pm	1 section moved to CRUCIFIX CORNER and 1 section to USNA Redoubt.	Appx.
	23/7/16		Remaining moved to USNA REDOUBT. Section at CRUCIFIX CORNER moved up to support 1st R.War.R. Heavily shelled in trench. 1 Officer killed. 10 ORs wounded – only two guns reached front trench. One section from USNA moving up.	Appx.
	24/7/16		out to LA BOISELLE.	
	25/7/16		Two teams sent from USNA to relieve front line guns. Guns and support bombing attack by 11th R.War.R. Lt POYNTING killed and 2 ORs wounded.	Appx. Appx.
	26/7/16		Lt BENNETT's body brought from trenches and buried in British Cemetery on Albert Road at W24C.8.3. Day fairly quiet.	Appx. Appx.
	27/7/16		Relieved by 36th M.G. Coy. and moved to billets in BOUZINCOURT. Lt POYNTING'S body buried at W24C.8.3.	Appx.
BOUZINCOURT	28/7/16	2.30pm	Moved by motor buses to COULANVILLERS. Transport moved by road; staying the night near TALMAS.	Appx.
	29/7/16		No work done. Transport arrived in evening.	Appx.
	30/7/16		Gun cleaning and overhaul.	Appx.
	31/7/16		Gun cleaning and repairs.	Appx.

Arthur [signature] 2/Lt for Capt.
Comd. 143 M.G. Coy.

143rd Brigade
48th Division

143rd BRIGADE MACHINE GUN COMPANY

AUGUST 1 9 1 6 ::::::

WAR DIARY or INTELLIGENCE SUMMARY

Army Form C. 2118

(Erase heading not required.)

Instructions regarding War Diaries and Intelligence Summaries are contained in F.S. Regs., Part II. and the Staff Manual respectively. Title Pages will be prepared in manuscript.

Place	Date	Hour	Summary of Events and Information	Remarks and references to Appendices
COULONVILLERS	1/8/16		Cleaning and overhaul of guns and equipment. Belts emptied & dried.	Nil.
Ref MAP. LENS II. 1/100.000 S.A.	2/8/16	6-8 a.m.	Route march. 9.30 a.m. Inspection of Company, followed by gun drill. Lecture on First Aid and Elementary dressings.	Nil.
	3/8/16	6.30 - 8 a.m.	Route march. 9.30 a.m. Drawing. Lecture on First Aid - and practical application.	Nil.
	4/8/16	6 - 8 a.m.	Route march. 9.30 a.m. Gun drill. Range finding and judging distance with human targets	Nil.
	5/8/16	6 - 8 a.m.	Company drill. Baths. Very hot.	Nil.
	6/8/16	12 noon	Church parade.	Nil.
	7/8/16	4 a.m. - 11 a.m.	Route march and guns belted on range.	Nil.
	8/8/16	9 a.m.	Overhauling guns &c. Packing limbers.	Nil.
GEZAINCOURT.	9/8/16.	4.55 a.m.	Moved from COULONVILLERS. via BEAUMETZ. FIENVILLERS. to GEZAINCOURT. arriving 12 noon. Company in bivouac.	Nil.
LEALVILLERS	10/8/16	6 a.m.	Moved from GEZAINCOURT via BEAUVAL. BEAUQUESNE. ARQUEVES to LEALVILLERS. Company in billets.	Nil.
Ref MAP. LENS II 1/100.000 6 G.	11/8/16	11 a.m.	Cleaning guns, overhauling kit. Smoke helmets &c.	Nil.
	12/8/16	10 a.m.	Gun drill and close order drill.	Nil.
	13/8/16	9.30 a.m.	Church parade. 2 guns taking part in demonstration attack at BELLE EGLISE	Nil.
BOUZAINCOURT	14/8/16	7.45 a.m.	Move from LEALVILLERS to bivouac at BOUZAINCOURT arriving 10.30 a.m.	Nil.
	15/8/16	9.30 a.m.	Parade for gun cleaning and belt overhauling. Lt O'DONNELL went up to line in training to arrange taking over from 144th Machine Gun Coy.	Nil.
MAP. OVILLERS 57D.SE 4 1/10.000	16/8/16		Relieved 144th M.G. Coy. in Trenches N of OVILLERS. 12 guns went into line and in support. 4 guns in reserve at Headquarters in OVILLERS Post (ref. W 16 B.4.6.)	Nil.

1875 Wt. W593/826 1,000,000 4/15 J.B.C. & A. A.D.S.S./Forms/C. 2118.

Army Form C. 2118

WAR DIARY
or
INTELLIGENCE SUMMARY
(Erase heading not required.)

Instructions regarding War Diaries and Intelligence Summaries are contained in F. S. Regs., Part II. and the Staff Manual respectively. Title Pages will be prepared in manuscript.

Place	Date	Hour	Summary of Events and Information	Remarks and references to Appendices
MAP. OVILLERS. 1/5000.	17/8/16		4 guns of M.M.G. action and 8 guns (Hotchkiss) of 1st Queens Own Yorkshire Dragoons attached to 143" M.G Coy during present operations.	Nil.
	18/8/16	5 p.m.	143rd INF. BDE attacked German line X2A 22. 43. 65. 76. 96. X2B 06. 48. 59 capturing and consolidating same. 2 M.Gs at THORSBY WESTLAND STREETS (X7B 29) fired rapid for 30 minutes from ZERO on German trenches X1B18. 39. 59 and second line also R31D 26. 35. 64. 74. and directly up MOQUET VALLEY. Several excellent targets were obtained in the region of X2A 19. 27. 29. 2 guns at X2C11 fired steadily on region of R32C 31. 33. 56. 65. 91. Guns at X8A 46 kept a steady fire on trench R32A 30. 34. 26. 2 guns at CONISTON POST (X7A 2.3) also kept a barrage across MOQUET VALLEY CAPT ELKINGTON A.D wounded. LT O'DONNELL takes command. The whole operation was most successful. and about 500 prisoners were taken.	Nil. Nil.
	19/8/16		During previous night and continued during this morning the 143rd Inf. Bde. bombed up 22 25 – 65 46 - 76 79. 143rd INF. BDE less two battalions and M.G Coy relieved by 144th INF. BDE and the M.G. Coy placed under orders of B.G.C this brigade.	Nil.
	20/8/16		The guns were disposed in positions from which they enfiladed the German trenches opposite R31D.	
	21/8/16		The 144th INF. BDE attacked at noon on the line R32C 15 R31D 81. X1B18 X1A98 R31C 90 R31D 30. 62. 84. which attack was in at 6 p.m. they again attacked the line R32C 31. X2A 79. R32C 91. This attack was only partially successful. The main successful. The 143" M.G Coy gave heavy supporting fire on German support lines R31D 07. 26 25. 64. 60. 79. 98 also in the region of R32C 58.	Nil.
	22/8/16		Day fairly quiet. Made arrangements for relief on 23rd	Nil.
	23/8/16		During forenoon handed over and were relieved by guns of 8th M.G. SQUADRON from positions in AUTHUILLE WOOD and in	

1875 Wt. W.593/826 1,000,000 4/15 I.B.C. & A. A.D.S.S./Forms/C. 2118.

Army Form C. 2118

WAR DIARY
or
INTELLIGENCE SUMMARY
(Erase heading not required.)

Instructions regarding War Diaries and Intelligence Summaries are contained in F.S. Regs., Part II. and the Staff Manual respectively. Title Pages will be prepared in manuscript.

Place	Date	Hour	Summary of Events and Information	Remarks and references to Appendices
MAP OVILLERS 1/5000	23/8/16		Continued. In the afternoon we relieved guns of 144th M.G. Coy on night of line. New dispositions then were - 4 guns in the line. 2 guns in support in OVILLERS and the remaining guns in support at USNA REDOUBT	App
	24/8/16		Nothing of importance. Local relief of teams in line.	App
	25/8/16		Nothing of importance.	App
	26/8/16		Attack by 7th Brigade on our left. Barrage of German third line S. of THIEPVAL successfully carried out. Overhead support fire by 143rd and 145th M.G. Coys. German communication trenches in rear of objective. Lt. AREND left to join 32nd M. Gun Coy. on admin of objective.	App
	27/8/16		Attack by 145th Brigade on line R 32 6 9, to 33, & by 143 ⊙ Bde (5th R Ham Regt.) on line R 32 & 23.25.14.03 to R 32 6 9 1. 2 Guns pushed forward; ① to Pt 14 SKYLINE TRENCH & ② to X 2 B 98. to protect flanks of attack. Attack on left successful on the right 1 bay lost direction; objective was reached and prisoners taken, but garrison being insufficient to hold it we withdrew to original line. To counter attack guns heavily shelled but not reduced in strength.	App
			2/Lt. T. BLAKE taken on strength.	

Army Form C. 2118

WAR DIARY
or
INTELLIGENCE SUMMARY

(Erase heading not required.)

Instructions regarding War Diaries and Intelligence Summaries are contained in F.S. Regs., Part II. and the Staff Manual respectively. Title Pages will be prepared in manuscript.

Place	Date	Hour	Summary of Events and Information	Remarks and references to Appendices
Ref ENSH	28.8.16	6 a.m.	Horse 143 Infy. Bde. relieved by 74th Infy. Bde. 2 Infy. Bde. M. Gun Coy. relief completed by 9.30 a.m. & then proceeded to VARENNES. Lieut. GRUNDY assumed to command	
MAP 57 S.E. 1/20000	29.8.16	8 a.m.	Moved to AUTHIE.	
4 LEN 11	30.8.16		Inspection and cleaning of guns & gun stores, hampered by continual rain.	
MAP	31.8.16		Kit & clothing inspection & issue of clean & new clothing Baths.	

B. O'Donnell Lt.
O.C. 143 M. Gun Coy
31.8.16.

48th. DIVISION

143rd. INFANTRY BDE.

143rd. MACHINE GUN COMPANY

SEPTEMBER 1916.

Vol 9

Confidential

WAR DIARY.
143rd.
MACHINE GUN Cº.

1st September, 1916 to 30th September, 1916.

VOLUME. 9.

Army Form C. 2118

WAR DIARY
or
INTELLIGENCE SUMMARY

(Erase heading not required.)

Instructions regarding War Diaries and Intelligence Summaries are contained in F.S. Regs., Part II. and the Staff Manual respectively. Title Pages will be prepared in manuscript.

Place	Date	Hour	Summary of Events and Information	Remarks and references to Appendices
AUTHIE LEN F 5.	1.9.16		Gun cleaning; issue of gun stores; baths.	A.O'D
—do—	2.9.16	10.30 a.m	Moved from AUTHIE to THIÈVRES. Billeted at the Mairie	A.O'D
	3.9.16	11.30 am	Church Parade with 1/8 R. War. R.	A.O'D
	4.9.16	9 am	Rained all day. Gun cleaning, stoppages and mechanism in billets. Early parade cancelled	A.O'D
	5.9.16	6.30 am	Route March Thievres-Sarton-Mariens-Thievres. Belt cleaning and stripping. Classes for reserve signallers	A.O'D
	6.9.16	6.30 am	Cleaning parade. Army Commander Gen Gough inspected 1/8 Qu War R. did not come to us. Gun drill	A.O'D
	7.9.16	6.30 am	Arms and Squad Drill. Gun drill Indication and Recognition of Targets. Inoculations	A.O'D
	8.9.16	6.30 am	Prepared Range landscape target miniature figures. Firing guns and revolvers on range. Inoculation	A.O'D
	9.9.16	6.30 am	Route March Thievres-Mariens-Sarton-Thievres. Stoppages mechanism. Inoculation	A.O'D
	10.9.16	12 noon	Church Parade	R.E.PS
BRETEL LENS II MAP D 5.	11.9.16	2.30 p.m	Moved from THIÈVRES to BRETEL	NKS
	12.9.16	6.30am	Arms Drill. Gun cleaning, belt filling & physical training	NKS
	13.9.16	3.00 am	Physical training. Heavy rain all morning. Cleaning stations. Mechanism training. C.C. conference at Bde H.Q. C.C.	NKS

WAR DIARY
or
INTELLIGENCE SUMMARY

(Erase heading not required.)

Army Form C. 2118

Instructions regarding War Diaries and Intelligence Summaries are contained in F.S. Regs., Part II. and the Staff Manual respectively. Title Pages will be prepared in manuscript.

Place	Date	Hour	Summary of Events and Information	Remarks and references to Appendices
BRETEL LENS 11 D 5	14/9/16	6.30 am	Physical training, firing at moving target & table 8 & 16 Z B, officers on Staff Ride	
— do —	15/9/16	6.30 am	Physical training, firing on range 20 on 16 Z. Officers on Staff Ride	
— do —	16.9.16	8 am	Baths, Gun cleaning & inspection	
— do —	17.9.16	11 am	Church parade, address by G.O.C. Division to officers	
PROUVILLE LENS 11 B 5.	18.9.16	6.30 am	Moved from BRETEL to PROUVILLE. Weather very bad	
	19.9.16	9.30 am	Gun cleaning & clearing gun stores — Weather very bad	
	20.9.16	9.30 am	Weather still bad, lectures, stoppages	
	21.9.16	7.30 am	Inspection of Gas Helmets, Lectures on transportation. Precautions against enemy fire & "Open fighting"	
	22.9.16	7.30 am	Short route march, still much rain. Physical drill, attack scheme	
	23.9.16	9.0 am	Attack scheme with advance guard, advance guard, one with before. Good training for Gas Masks. Useful lessons deducted	
GRIMONT LENS 11 A/5 B		2.30 pm	Company moved to GRIMONT. Very small village of 350 souls including refugees. No water invillage, infantry difficult to obtain owing to billets	

Army Form C. 2118

WAR DIARY
or
INTELLIGENCE SUMMARY

(Erase heading not required.)

Instructions regarding War Diaries and Intelligence Summaries are contained in F. S. Regs., Part II. and the Staff Manual respectively. Title Pages will be prepared in manuscript.

Place	Date	Hour	Summary of Events and Information	Remarks and references to Appendices
MAP/10000 LENS/II				
HEUZECOURT LENS 1:MAP	24.9.16	12 noon	Church Parades.	
Ref Map/10000 LENS 11	25.9.16	8 a.m – 2 p.m	2 sections engaged in Brigade scheme for training in Coy. Major Ops:- barring of orders, co-operation & communications. Difficulties encountered:- Mounted orderlies would be necessary. Mobilization table strength of a Machine Gun Coy. difficult to work with e.g. many more men are required to keep up supply of ammunition. Remainder of Coy engaged in gun cleaning, use of period scores, physical training.	H.Q.Ps
GRIMONT 4/5 B.				
BERMAVILLE 5/B.	26.9.16	8.30 a.m – 6 p.m	Company engaged in a Divisional tactical scheme - attack on BERMAVILLE. 1 section attached to Division. Some 3 a.m soon as cavalry patrols reported MT. RENAULT FARM RIDGE clear of enemy, this section came into action on limbers & consolidated, & held against counter attacks. Weather very good.	
GRIMONT	27.9.16	8 a.m – 2 p.m	do for 25.9.16.	
	28.9.16	8 a.m – 2 p.m	do for 25.9.16 for 2 sections. Remainder of Coy. attached to two infantry companies defending BERMAVILLE used to protect flanks and hold roads & to cover withdrawal of villages into a after front has been taken (Divisional tactical scheme)	
GRENAS 5/E	29.9.16	9.30 a.m	Company moved to GRENAS.	
SOUASTRE 5/E	30.9.16	11.30 a.m	Company moved to SOUASTRE.	

H.P. Manton
OC 143rd Bde. M. G. Coy

1875 Wt. W593/826 1,000,000 4/15 J.B.C. & A. A.D.S.S./Forms/C. 2118.

Vol 10

VOL. X.

WAR DIARY.

143rd MGC.

From ~ 1st Oct.

To ~ 31st Oct.

Army Form C. 2118.

WAR DIARY
or
INTELLIGENCE SUMMARY

(Erase heading not required.)

Instructions regarding War Diaries and Intelligence Summaries are contained in F.S. Regs., Part II and the Staff Manual respectively. Title Pages will be prepared in manuscript.

Place	Date	Hour	Summary of Events and Information	Remarks and references to Appendices
SOUASTRE MAP (D22). 57D N.E. Ed. 26. 1/20000.	1.10.16		LT. O'DONNELL to hospital (Influenza). 2 LT. F.C.P. STANTON assumed command. 6.64 Lacton Officers made a reconnaissance of HEBUTERNE sector between K 11.c.2.0 to K 10 A 7.9. & arranged details of relief with O.C. 98th M. Gun 80. Time reverted to legal time.	
HEBUTERNE	2.10.16	9.30 a.m.	Company relieved 98th M. Gun Co. Also guns in front line; three guns in support line; three guns in support in HEBUTERNE village. 1 section in Brigade reserve at SAILLY (J16). Weather bad. Lacton very quiet. Good alignment. Two guns of 1H 8 M. Gun Co. ordered to be relieved by us on our left between K 10 A 7.9 & K 3 D 25.40. Two good emplacements & dug outs.	
	3.10.16		(e.g. 1 gun now in support of HEBUTERNE. Keen on firing enemy sent over a few barrage rounds with Lewis Gun versa — occasionally silent our trenches. Own guns engaged enemy emplacements & dug out fire. Improved two emplacements & dug out & a straight trench.) Improved two emplacements were between our artillery commenced to cut enemy wire.	
	4.10.16		K 14 A 1.7 (SERRE ROAD) and K 4 D 1.5 (GOMME COURT WOOD). Own guns trained on gaps made & fired when our patrols were in to keep gaps open. Enemy quiet.	
	5.10.16	9.30 a.m.	Company (less Lacton) relieved by 51st M. Gun Co. Lacton still in line between K 9 B 5.8 and K 3 D 2.5. CAPT GRUNDY returned from leave and assumed command.	

2449 Wt. W14957/M90 750,000 1/16 J.B.C. & A. Forms/C.2118/12.

Army Form C. 2118.

WAR DIARY
or
INTELLIGENCE SUMMARY
(Erase heading not required.)

Instructions regarding War Diaries and Intelligence Summaries are contained in F.S. Regs., Part II. and the Staff Manual respectively. Title Pages will be prepared in manuscript.

Place	Date	Hour	Summary of Events and Information	Remarks and references to Appendices
Reference Map.57.D N.E 1/20000 Ed. 2.6. ST AMAND D 9-10.	5.10.16	12.15 p.m	Company (two & Sect.) proceeded to ST AMAND. Conditions owing to concentration of troops. Lectures on gas mine during night. Gun artillery heavy activity at enemy mine.	
	6.10.16	9.0 am	Gun clearing and repacking of artillery ammunition. Sects attached to L.T. BROMHALL arrived to take over 2nd in command. Gun artillery in line we moved activity steady — also trench mortars very active. Two new machine gun positions observed to explode from K 3 D 66.75 to E 28 central.	
	7.10.16	9.0 am	O.C and 2 Section officers reconnoitred line with view of hurrying forward the new attack on GOMMECOURT. Batteries chosen for K 3 A & C. Company at ST AMAND carried on training – grenades, physical drill, immediate action.	
	8.10.16	9 am	Baths for available men of company. 2 Sections at work building emplacements chosen yesterday. Sector constructed to find and take them engaged playing & confirmed officers had to observe enemy operation on this front.	

LT. O'DONNELL returned from leave today.

WAR DIARY
or
INTELLIGENCE SUMMARY

(Erase heading not required.)

Army Form C. 2118.

Instructions regarding War Diaries and Intelligence Summaries are contained in F. S. Regs., Part II. and the Staff Manual respectively. Title Pages will be prepared in manuscript.

Place	Date	Hour	Summary of Events and Information	Remarks and references to Appendices
ST AMAND France	9/10/16		A and 'B' Section marched out to trenches opposite GOMMECOURT and continued the building of 8 other emplacements and 8 small niches to hold spare gun numbers in the parapet. Another 15 yards of track emplacement. These niches were linked up and revetted with expanded metal and revetted with expanded metal 8 men from each battalion in the Brigade became attached to the company every day for instruction. Table alongside being enlarging large to enable the company to carry into action the necessary materials for 18 guns.	JWB
Do.	10/10/16		Lt O'DONNELL returned to hospital. Company inspected company by fighting over and General allocation made of equipment. Gas clearing and lectures took place for any probable advance.	JWB
Do.	11/10/16		Lectures took for immaterial duties - inspected company lectured by Officer on tactical movements on GOMMECOURT WOOD.	JWB
Do.	12/10/16		Gun drill. Tactical exercise "Defending the flank of a village" Demonstration and Practice of "Overhead and Barrage fire by tens.	JWB
Do.	13/10/16		Buffs in the open. O/C took men rested billeting cook on the farm. Marching, bomb'ing and gas.	JWB
Do.	14/10/16		Tactical Exercise taking a position in the open surround from of guns. Gas Drill and Arms Drill. Arrested men collected in Voluntary. March Discipline. Church Parade.	JWB
Do.	15/10/16		Infantry Drill and Physical Training.	JWB
Do.	16/10/16			JWB
Do.	17/10/16		Sanitary Practical Marching Reconnaissance by Lieut. Elsworth and the work of action in the open.	JWB
Do.	18/10/16		Men attached from Battalions rejoined their Corps of Various Battalions and Bomb fighting and Mechanical Course of Various Battalions and Bomb throwing commenced.	JWB

Army Form C. 2118.

WAR DIARY
or
INTELLIGENCE SUMMARY
(Erase heading not required.)

Instructions regarding War Diaries and Intelligence Summaries are contained in F. S. Regs, Part II. and the Staff Manual respectively. Title Pages will be prepared in manuscript.

Place	Date	Hour	Summary of Events and Information	Remarks and references to Appendices
ST AMAND	19/10/16		The word "Meteor Cholera" to marking ribbon for a march from billets in ST AMAND as detailed from "march Order" when billeting party sent on for next billets are arrived.	9473
D°	20/10/16		Company moved from ST AMAND to GRAND RULLENCOURT.	9473
GRAND RULLENCOURT	21/10/16		Company rested and wire tested	9473
D°	22/10/16		Church parade.	9473
D°	23/10/16		Re-fitting and preparation for move. Football match. Concert	9473
D°	24/10/16		Transport and officer chargers moved with all gun equipment available stores to FAVIERS	9473
D°	25/10/16		Transport moved on to FRANVILLERS. Company marched to ST OUEN & were billeted by French Motor Lorries to FRANVILLERS.	9473
D°	26/10/16		Company and transport marched to BECOURT & encamped in huts	9473
BECOURT	27/10/16		Company arrived in encamped in huts	9473
D°	28/10/16		Company on Brigade fatigue and practice packing mules & officer reconnaissance ground of probable operation in view	9473
D°	29/10/16		Company on Brigade fatigue and practice packing mules to officers reconnaissance ground of probable operation in view	9473
D°	30/10/16		Company on Brigade fatigue and practice packing mules to officers reconnaissance ground of probable occupation in view	9473
D°	31/10/16		Company on Brigade fatigue and new personnel trained on guns. 3 officers reconnaissance ground of probable occupation in view.	9473

WAR DIARY.

143 Machine Gun Coy.

November 1st — November 30th
1916

Army Form C. 2118.

WAR DIARY
or
INTELLIGENCE SUMMARY
(Erase heading not required.)

Instructions regarding War Diaries and Intelligence Summaries are contained in F. S. Regs., Part II. and the Staff Manual respectively. Title Pages will be prepared in manuscript.

Place	Date	Hour	Summary of Events and Information	Remarks and references to Appendices
ALBERT	Nov. 1		Company moved from BECOURT CAMP to ALBERT. Billets in RUE DU BRAY arrived 8 P.M.	JCB
ALBERT	Nov. 2		Gen cleaning.	JCB
FRICOURT	Nov. 3		Company moved to FRICOURT. Bivouaced near LONELY TRENCH arrived 12 noon. B.O. made a tour of Coys M.G. LINE. Running from DESTREMENT FARM to about FORK of ROAD 800 yds S.W. of EAUCOURT L'ABBAYE.	JCB
FRICOURT	Nov. 4		B.C.'D Section moved to MARTINPUICH and on the night of 4/5 were taken to Coys line by officers to prepare shelters from which to work on positions in Coys line. A Section worked on consolidation of emp't at LONELY TRENCH.	JCB
FRICOURT	Nov. 5		B.C.+ D. before in Coys line.	JCB
FRICOURT	Nov. 6		Building shelters. A Section went to consolidating LONELY TRENCH	JCB
FRICOURT	Nov. 7		Building shelters. A Section consolidating LONELY TRENCH	JCB
FRICOURT	Nov. 8		Company H.Q. and A Section moved to Hulluch. 2 of Contalmaison Village. Section bombarded between 7 and 9 P.M. one dugout hit, no casualties. H.Q. and A Section Nº1 moved back to LONELY TRENCH Station from the Coys line. A new relieved by 145 M.G. Coy on a marksman took to LONELY TRENCH. A Section consolidating dugouts and shellproof Sergeants Mess in MARTINPUICH. 1 Ot Killed and 1 O.R. (?) on Bazenbin - MARTINPUICH RD.	JCB
FRICOURT	Nov. 9		Company less A Section resting.	JCB
FRICOURT	Nov. 10		Company at LONELY TRENCH bathed at BECOURT MILL.	JCB
MARTINPUICH	Nov. 11		Company less Transport moved up to MARTINPUICH and relieved 144 and 143 M.G. Coys from LIGNY-THILLOY. M.14.d. 85 from the point. 3 volunteer during relief.	JCB
MARTINPUICH	Nov. 12		N.Q. Dugout and mess in neighbourhood shelled with H.E. on shrapnel to Coy Cooker opened fire in MARTINPUICH	JCB

WAR DIARY or INTELLIGENCE SUMMARY

Army Form C. 2118.

(Erase heading not required.)

Place	Date	Hour	Summary of Events and Information	Remarks and references to Appendices
MARTINPUICH	13/11/16		During early morning our artillery were very active in a Chinese attack arranged for the purpose of assisting the 5th Army in their attack on BEAUMONT HAMEL. Our front and support line was heavily shelled during the day. Our gun chambers completely denied and some able to dig themselves out and low any cover than shelter was also secured before midnight. During the night one of the men was shelled and the gun teaches was withdrawn. No casualties were reported.	N.B.
MARTINPUICH	14/11/16		Owing to an attack by the 149 Inf Bde our guns out a considerable amount of relieving at a range of about 1000 yards. No enemies seen.	N.B.
MARTINPUICH	15/11/16		Day quiet. 6 enfantryment by 144 and 145 Bays night of 15-16. D'Section refurnished in MARTINPUICH. according to Brigade Orders general was also safe whilst in celler. Company moved to CONTALMAISON.	N.B.
CONTALMAISON	16/11/16		MARTINPUICH shelled heavily. Casualties to Company Nil. D'Section improved accommodation and had L formed aban aft. Company alan aft. Designs/or standard Tables & forms of hut by Capt. Furn were executed in timber = Muskills/abor-mad Table in larger were executed in timber = Muskills/abor-mad Table in larger Brigade rep-on and so on. moved to A5th DROP CAMP worked	N.B.
do	17/11/16		Company furnished and informed A.S.C.	N.B.
do	18/11/16		Company marched to talking but were too wet muddy.	N.B.
do	19/11/16		Construction of cart continued and was employed in building tables and forms &c.	N.B.
do	20/11/16		Coy moved to other hub so got hut furnished, work amounted, stories & Drawn out.	N.B.
do	21/11/16		Company returned at BECOURT. Company at work on improvement of hub meanwhile.	N.B.
do	22/11/16		Improvement of units quarters continued.	N.B.
do	23/11/16		Company moved to New Brigade 145 Camp. SHELTER WOOD N. of FRICOURT. This camp is especially built for Brigade Details. 6 huts to take 25 men, 1 officers Mess and sleeping, 1 Orderly Room and Stores &c.	N.B.

Army Form C. 2118.

WAR DIARY
or
INTELLIGENCE SUMMARY

(Erase heading not required.)

Instructions regarding War Diaries and Intelligence Summaries are contained in F. S. Regs., Part II. and the Staff Manual respectively. Title Pages will be prepared in manuscript.

Place	Date	Hour	Summary of Events and Information	Remarks and references to Appendices
MARTINPUICH	24/11/16		Company relieved 1st M.G. Coy in line and 2 Coy's positions during the night owing to shell fire, two parties were killed which delayed the relief considerably. The men came only took up their own guns and of one party, the tripods commentries etc of company to be relieved were left as first stores. 6 Mules were killed and 2 guns were destroyed and eight casualties occurred by shell fire while relieving.	PM3
do	25/11/16		Company in the line. Canteen opened in MARTINPUICH. During night 1 gun fired on BAPAUME RD.	PM3
do	26/11/16		Company in the line.	PM3
do	27/11/16		Company in the line. Conference of Company Commanders with Lt.Col. M.G.O. at VILLA WOOD. BAZENTIN LE PETIT. Lt R.G. CARNALL wounded at 4.30 PM	PM3
do	28/11/16		Company in the line. Transport report 6 sick L.D removed to Vet. Hospital. 11 Deficiences in animal transport.	PM3
do	29/11/16		Night 28-29 Jan of 145-264 E (attached for occupation to 141 M.G Coy) at range about 2000 on LITTLEWOOD and from N.E. of MARTINPUICH.	PM3
do	30/11/16		Company in the line. 2 gun firing in the night on overs fire.	PM3

J.V. Bromhead Lieut./A Capt.
Comdg. 143 M.G.Coy.

2449 Wt. W14957/M90 750,000 1/16 J.B.C. & A. Forms/C.2118/12.

War Diary

143rd Machine Gun Coy.

From Dec 1st 1916. To Dec 31st 1916.

Army Form C. 2118.

WAR DIARY
or
INTELLIGENCE SUMMARY

(Erase heading not required.)

Instructions regarding War Diaries and Intelligence Summaries are contained in F.S. Regs., Part II. and the Staff Manual respectively. Title Pages will be prepared in manuscript.

Place	Date	Hour	Summary of Events and Information	Remarks and references to Appendices
MARTINPUICH	1/12/16		Company in the line. Endeavoured to get hut from in 3rd stage was made which by some tags. Front impracticable owing to shell torn and the condition of the ground. Dominie workers fixed by Pole. Floored more successful.	App 3
do	2/12/16		Company in line. Relief started at 12.30 pm completed by 11 pm. Two fields killed, two horses wounded by 2 guerilla shells. Camouflet etc now ready to the neighbours together.	App 2
CONTALMAISON	3/12/16		Company at rest in SHELTER WOOD. CONTALMAISON	App 3
do	4/12/16		Company back and clear clothing issued. Company visited Div. Gunnery Party. Shade state not started which is designed to return division at a moment's notice. Report of names of company and men as he called when	App 2
do	5/12/16		Church & Egerton Parade under Divisional Padre. Horse exhibition to Camp.	App 3
do	6/12/16		Company took on line from this M.G. Coy. 8 Sec Australian Tunl in MARTINPUICH. Relief completed no incident. 12 Sevens Coming Coy. Company up to former keep by working on pumps supplies etc. greatly relieved the fatigue of that relieving section.	App 3
do	7/12/16		Company in line.	App 3
do	8/12/16		Brigadier obliged the line to be in to the sought tank about to again visited R. Sector front system also the Sec. a 28 SAPS & a thought had one here to many.	App 2

Army Form C. 2118.

WAR DIARY
or
INTELLIGENCE SUMMARY

(Erase heading not required.)

Instructions regarding War Diaries and Intelligence Summaries are contained in F. S. Regs., Part II. and the Staff Manual respectively. Title Pages will be prepared in manuscript.

Place	Date	Hour	Summary of Events and Information	Remarks and references to Appendices
MARTINPUICH	9/12/16		Capt Church recommend our own positions and communication with the Brigades received the morning as no information	9/13
	10/12/16		Company relieved by 1st M.W. Relief completed 1.25 hours no casualties occurred. Party to one in the morning in the of leaving the Trenches as it was so wet and although the company was relieved Coming off duty one man reported sick from the Co's Lewis Gun section and was sent of some of company. Each team casing the clearing to see their team either made a contribution to the hiring of G.S. Limber waggon waggons were sent out also to carry the equipment and see, except Lewis Gun and the shelter over was unfed who the to the mens' clearing stations. The company arrived at Scotland Camp just from the [illegible] line.	9/13
CONTALMAISON	11/12/16		Company at rest in Scotland Camp	9/13
	12/12/16		Company at Baths, Pig Latrines and cleaning Camp	9/13
	13/12/16		Officers attend conferences etc	9/13
	14/12/16		Improvement on Camp Latrine and cleaning	9/13
	15/12/16		Company moved to MILLENCOURT arrived [illegible] and marched over to M.E. Coy and to MILLENCOURT and a 2615 to Camp Somewhere	9/13
MILLENCOURT	16/12/16		Company started cleaning house allotments	9/13
	17/12/16		Company started for attack	
	18/12/16		Gun and equipment cleaning	9/13
	19/12/16		Gun and equipment cleaning and camp improvements	9/13

2449 Wt. W14957/Mg0 750,000 1/16 J.B.C. & A. Forms/C.2118/12

Army Form C. 2118.

WAR DIARY
or
INTELLIGENCE SUMMARY
(Erase heading not required.)

Instructions regarding War Diaries and Intelligence Summaries are contained in F.S. Regs, Part II. and the Staff Manual respectively. Title Pages will be prepared in manuscript.

Place	Date	Hour	Summary of Events and Information	Remarks and references to Appendices
MILLENCOURT	20/12/16		Machine Gun Training and Camp Improvements.	P.D.
"	21/12/16		Baths for whole company. Belt filling and gun and equipment cleaning.	P.D.
"	22/12/16		Training and Camp Improvement. Harness Shed erected for Transport.	P.D.
"	23/12/16		Training and Camp Improvement.	P.D.
"	24/12/16		No Parades. Company Concert with Band.	P.D.
"	25/12/16		No Parades. Company Dinner.	P.D.
"	26/12/16		Company Training and Fatigue.	P.D.
"	27/12/16		Section Training and Fatigue.	P.D.
"	28/12/16		Company left MILLENCOURT 10.50 a.m. and marched to billets at WARLOY-BAILLON.	P.D.
WARLOY	29/12/16		Fatigues, road cleaning etc.	P.D.
"	30/12/16		Gun Testing on Range. Transport Standing and Harness Room improved.	P.D.
"	31/12/16		Firing Trench constructed on Range for firing practice.	P.D.

P. Booker Lieut. for Capt.
Cmdg. M.G. Coy.
143rd

War Diary.

143
~~145~~ Machine Gun Coy

January 1st to January 31st 1917

Army Form C. 2118.

WAR DIARY
or
INTELLIGENCE SUMMARY
(Erase heading not required.)

Instructions regarding War Diaries and Intelligence Summaries are contained in F. S. Regs., Part II. and the Staff Manual respectively. Title Pages will be prepared in manuscript.

Place	Date	Hour	Summary of Events and Information	Remarks and references to Appendices
WARLOY	1/1/17		Trench inspected. Gen. cleaning the morning day.	JCB
	2/1/17		Trench inspected. Gun drill on range.	JCB
	3/1/17		Gun drill, infantry drill and general inspection of trench.	JCB
	4/1/17		Route march. Gen. trench inspecting drill and general cleaning.	JCB
	5/1/17		Company had orders that for morning off on the Divisional orders inspect inspection by E.O. Company, so march, going on range as morning, Company suggested held on that or range. Part go to LAVIEVILLE to cause inspection by Brigadier in morning and so in afternoon the company was formed in sight of the Brigade.	JCB
	6/1/17			JCB
	7/1/17		Back in morning. Football match in afternoon.	JCB
	8/1/17		Company marched from WARLOY to MERICOURT L'ABBAYE and then marched to BETTINCOURT.	JCB
	9/1/17		Continued resting and inspection held. Brigade order to all units (see later sheet attached) re a Field Bde order to v. Loan ready hiding.	JCB

2449 Wt. W14957/Mgo 750,000 1/16 J.B.C. & A. Forms/C.2118/12.

Army Form C. 2118.

WAR DIARY
or
INTELLIGENCE SUMMARY

(Erase heading not required.)

Instructions regarding War Diaries and Intelligence Summaries are contained in F. S. Regs., Part II. and the Staff Manual respectively. Title Pages will be prepared in manuscript.

Place	Date	Hour	Summary of Events and Information	Remarks and references to Appendices
BETTINCOURT	10/1/17		Route march. Infantry drill and advanced Machine gun work.	PCB
"	11/1/17		Route march and advanced Machine gun work	PCB
"	12/1/17		Route march and advanced Machine gun work. Transfer of motor limbers & drill.	PCB
"	13/1/17		Party returned from LANEVILLE after course with Motor Machine Gun Battery. Lt BROMHALL & Lieut. Lt BROMHALL attended conference at Div. HqQrs.	PCB
"	14/1/17		Church Parade in the afternoon.	PCB
"	15/1/17		Firing on range. In the evening Lt BROMHALL declined to take company on system of training as commanded by G.O.C.	PCB
"	16.1.17		Company practice actions.	PCB
"	17.1.17		Transport inspected by Col. Roberts O/c N9 Div. Train. Reports "Excellent". Company go route march. Lieut Blake goes on leave to U.K.	PCB
"	18.1.17		Training under fiction Officers. Lt T.C. Bromhall to Paris on leave	PCB
"	19.1.17		Training under fiction Officers, gun drill, gun cleaning, gun firing on range. Ball of ammn. drill continues.	PCB
"	20.1.17		Sections practice of firing with return from limbers. 2/Lt GREGSON. H. to hospital	PCB
"	21.1.17		No work done. Church parade. N.C.O's fire on range. Company passed.	PCB

Army Form C. 2118.

WAR DIARY
or
INTELLIGENCE SUMMARY
(Erase heading not required.)

Instructions regarding War Diaries and Intelligence Summaries are contained in F.S. Regs., Part II. and the Staff Manual respectively. Title Pages will be prepared in manuscript.

Place	Date	Hour	Summary of Events and Information	Remarks and references to Appendices
BETTENCOURT	22.1.17		Company carried out drill attack in conjunction with the infantry in the neighbourhood of HALLENCOURT. The Rgt taken by the Bog. Eight guns proceeded with the first wave of the infantry, their objective being the German support line, with orders to push forward into the German reserve line as soon as reports or personal reconnaissance proved it to be consolidated. Remaining eight guns were held in Brigade reserve. Subsequent orders should the eight guns in Brigade reserve go forward and take up position in front of the German reserve line (passing through guns already there), the eight guns in the German reserve line would automatically become Brigade reserve.	903
"	23.1.17		Training under Section officers. Lecture during the evening on "Intensive fire" by Capt. G.K.O. Grundy to N.C.Os.	903
"	24.1.17		Company clean guns and stores. Limbers packed. Remounts drawn to complete establishment of animals.	903
"	25.1.17		Transport and Billetting party of 1 Officer and 3 men move off for new area. Q.M. Billetted at ARGOEUVES. Company during day feature + making of gun bags for wet weather, made of tar cloth + waterproof sheets. Lecture during evening on Signalisation.	903
"	26.1.17		Transport continued to march. Billetted at AUBIGNY. Coy on fatigues.	903
"	27.1.17		Coy entrained at AIRAINES, detrained at CERISY + proceeded to billets in MERICOURT/SOMME. Billets occupied by French troops. Transport arrived at MERICOURT + the weather continued cold, all water in roads froze. Horses watered from stream. Ice previously had to be broken.	903
MERICOURT	28.1.17		Coy repair trestles and rest. N.B. Coy mobilised by Lt. J.G. Branhall on taking over of new line.	903

2449 Wt. W14957/Mg0 750,000 1/16 J.B.C. & A. Forms/C.2118/12.

Army Form C. 2118.

WAR DIARY
or
INTELLIGENCE SUMMARY
(Erase heading not required.)

Instructions regarding War Diaries and Intelligence Summaries are contained in F.S. Regs., Part II. and the Staff Manual respectively. Title Pages will be prepared in manuscript.

Place	Date	Hour	Summary of Events and Information	Remarks and references to Appendices
MERICOURT	30.1.17		Gun cleaning, also cleaning and packing of limbers	
MERICOURT	31.1.17		Coy moved to huts in ECLUSIER via ETINHEM-BRAY-SUZANNE	

Vol 14

WAR DIARY

143 MACHINE GUN COY

Oct 1st 1917 — Feb 28/18

Army Form C. 2118.

WAR DIARY
or
INTELLIGENCE SUMMARY

(Erase heading not required.)

Place	Date	Hour	Summary of Events and Information	Remarks and references to Appendices
	1/2/17		Company moved from FEUILLER with orders to take over some of NW of BIACHES prior to the French attack on that night. 2,000 rounds of S.A.A. on the BIACHES HERBECOURT RD arriving at the rendezvous at 3.30pm. Royal guides were sent with party from HERBECOURT and proceeded with us on a holding the ground to the relieving battalion. The Brigade front covered a number of strong points about on the East side of the river SOMME to about HAUT HALLU (N of the Royes) down the West bank of the River SOMME to a point half way through the village of BIACHES. This was under the Brigade HQ. This section on the BOMME we were South and Brigade front turned as in MAISONETTE. This was placed into 2 a battalion front, the reserve battalion was then by the staff on orders. An effort to attention at FEUILLER (Raised by staff officer) for Brigade front came but there was no effect any and Major Victoria under orders the command of 2/Lt SHOFREY (Right Sector) 2/Lt NORRIS (Left Sector) and Major HOOK (Reserve). The Brigade had small arms ammunition, bombs and rations were taken our by the balloon train down the fields and the relief was successfully completed without casualty by 12.30 AM the French are very pleased on account of the relief them	

Army Form C. 2118.

WAR DIARY
or
INTELLIGENCE SUMMARY
(Erase heading not required.)

Instructions regarding War Diaries and Intelligence Summaries are contained in F. S. Regs., Part II. and the Staff Manual respectively. Title Pages will be prepared in manuscript.

Place	Date	Hour	Summary of Events and Information	Remarks and references to Appendices
	1/5/17		[illegible handwritten notes regarding the battalion, Kaffir Wood, operations] (KUBOKO WOOD).	903
	2/5/17		Company was ordered to the line under command of 2nd Lt [illegible]. The Bgde that the rest of the Bn. could [illegible] the [illegible] to join the [illegible] Batt. the [illegible] at [illegible] to relieve them. [illegible] held the line [illegible] [illegible] [illegible] after ZERO. The scouts were returning along the [illegible] could see some huts [illegible] along the front [illegible] by the HARBONCOURT-PONCHES Rd. The [illegible] trenches along the old [illegible] from 8/9 Bgde, and were occupied by daybreak.	904
	3/5/17		Company in the Tr. Col. [illegible] [illegible] showing the enemy [illegible] [illegible] to carry out an attack along the line [illegible] [illegible] was available. The sick the following night	905

2449 Wt. W14957/M90 750,000 1/16 J.B.C. & A. Forms/C.2118/12.

Army Form C. 2118.

WAR DIARY
or
INTELLIGENCE SUMMARY

(Erase heading not required.)

Instructions regarding War Diaries and Intelligence Summaries are contained in F. S. Regs., Part II. and the Staff Manual respectively. Title Pages will be prepared in manuscript.

Place	Date	Hour	Summary of Events and Information	Remarks and references to Appendices
	4/2/17		Orders were issued to the OC that the Coy Guns supported by over the relief arriving. S.W. from TRENCHES. At 3.30PM the enemy opened up a barrage on the RIGHT Sector which was replied to with vigor. At about 4.30PM a rifle party of about 40 enemy advanced on our trenches but owing to the make up of return fire, few reached the trench. The Machine gun on the RIGHT Sector inflicted the advancing line a caused many casualties before both guns replied. The enemy withdrew, leaving the ground strewn during the attack. The ambulance advanced at 8 ac about 66791 1.B.11. about P. 62795 P. Pages P., 36696 P. Quelles Sector and G.231 P. Sector P., 32095 P. Guy P., 32320 P. Nawby P., movement.	JWB
	5/2/17		Company in the 2nd line, trenches every of assistance of Coy. to temporary positions. Infantry carrying party of 4/40 employed in carrying ammunition.	JWB
	6/2/17		Company in the 2nd line, RIGHT SECTOR. Tomorrow relieves about 6.15 the 1st and 2nd major suffered several severed off the 2nd severed off by kilbs of bodies. Doing a cold wet several met about 3.PM. the Relief was completed and the Coy was ordered for manoeuvre. RIGHT portion of the RIGHT SECTOR was evacuated to use owned by trench morter still fair, and fraction of the right our right of the will only after several down of man knew that then to become an affair with good shocks that the Branch began...	

WAR DIARY
or
INTELLIGENCE SUMMARY

(Erase heading not required.)

Army Form C. 2118.

Place	Date	Hour	Summary of Events and Information	Remarks and references to Appendices
	6/2/17		[illegible] from the air raid in [illegible] [illegible] low lift was responsible for this. One [illegible] [illegible] [illegible] down the [illegible] [illegible] to the [illegible] of the E[illegible] of this [illegible] [illegible] were a stray shell on his dugout.	JCB
	7/2/17		Company in the line. One section was attacked to 5th Company from the 145 Regt. Coy and arranged to [illegible] a [illegible] in [illegible] Scot on the night of 7/8. The relief was reported completed at 12.10 AM 8/2	JCB
	8/2/17		Company in line. Reserve section and Headquarters Coy	JCB
	9/2/17		Company in the line among enemy patrols [illegible]	JCB
	10/2/17		Company in the line. Lt Tho Company relief carried out its [illegible] and was located in [illegible] [illegible] [illegible] on [illegible] [illegible] of the Reserve and Biacmes (LEFT) Coy in a dugouts of course and by 12.0 midnight no casualties. Lieut Scones G.T. [illegible] from [illegible] on [illegible] leave 9/2 Lt [illegible] May G.T. left on [illegible].	JCB
	11/2/17		Company in the line.	
	12/2/17		Company in the line. [illegible] [illegible] for Div Conf[illegible] [illegible] G.O.C. notified Coy Commander that owing to the excellent work done by the machine gunners of this Coy during an enemy raid on [illegible] took that the [illegible] on [illegible] were [illegible]	JCB JCB

2449 Wt. W14957/M90 750,000 1/16 J.B.C. & A. Forms/C.2118/12.

WAR DIARY
or
INTELLIGENCE SUMMARY

Army Form C. 2118.

(Erase heading not required.)

Place	Date	Hour	Summary of Events and Information	Remarks and references to Appendices
	13.2.17		Sgt Bunce and two teams relieved by Sgt Gardner and two teams in the RIGHT SECTOR	JCB
	14.2.17		Company in the line. Lieut J C Boronski interviewed the Bde Major with respect to G.O. but found it at its best "the Battn Commander will use his own discretion as to the use of the machine gun and also order such defensive fire as he judges for the defence of the Salient and retaliation and offensive fire as conditions necessary". The first clause of this paragraph was made conditional on the Bde Major's translation and the personnel of the teams should be temporarily increased by attaching infantry sentries to the machine should the personnel of team not be sufficient to mount and machine so are required. Sgt 23084 Sp(?) McNeil J. team were awarded the M.M.	JCB
	15.2.17		Company in the line. 14 guns moved their stores to new position in Bde area	JCB
	16.2.17		Company in the line. One N.C.O. sent to Divl. Gas School. Three teams with 2/Lieut May moved into BIACHES SECTOR and issued three teams in that time. Anti-aircraft gun established	JCB
	17.2.17		Company in the line. Four new officers arrived viz 2/Lt Hayes A.A., 2/Lieut Heaton, G.D., 2/Lieut Sackipp D., and 2/Lieut James D.	JCB
	18.2.17		Company in the line. Relief of 3 teams in RESERVE by top 3 teams in the Lieut Thomas. 14 guns moving to its area as by completed accordingly.	JCB
	19.2.17		Company in the line	JCB
	20.2.17		Company in the line. Considerable aeroplane fire marked its barrage reference. Three quarters of a shot of tubes were removed in 24 hours.	JCB
	21.2.17		Company in the line. At this late, returns had to the return showing the numerical	JCB
	22.2.17		Company in the line. Sgt Gardner and stores team on RIGHT SECTOR relieved by Sgt Watts and two teams. Light shots issued to log. Teams in the line were immediately affected by Howitzers. The pack each carrying material field employed as many men who's to put them up in light of lines.	JCB

2449 Wt. W14957/Mgo 750,000 1/16 J.B.C. & A. Forms/C.2118/12

Army Form C. 2118.

WAR DIARY
or
INTELLIGENCE SUMMARY

(Erase heading not required.)

Instructions regarding War Diaries and Intelligence Summaries are contained in F. S. Regs., Part II and the Staff Manual respectively. Title Pages will be prepared in manuscript.

Place	Date	Hour	Summary of Events and Information	Remarks and references to Appendices
	23.x.17		Company in the line. Heavy barrage during from the SOUTH working up to BIACHES. Our S.O.S. fired on the barrage lines during the S.O.S.	
	24.x.17		Heavy barrage again early in the morning. Barrage object unknown. Sgt Bruce and three teams relieved Sgt Marshall and other teams in BIACHES	
	25.x.17		Two N.C.Os sent to CAMIERS Bridge building Coy, an attempt to enable transport to come up to Coy Hd Qrs splinter proof of enemy gun shell look-outs. Gas boy in certain operation in a fortnight attachments and 5 O.Rs were taken by the boy in return. 10 O.Rs of a mint situated character was removed. Branded and relieved.	
			Guide taken to Reserve gun positions & was to have been seen by company morning. Two aeroplanes are machine-gunning were fired conference of Div N.C.Os	
	26.x.17		2/Lt Shufford relieved 2/Lt Hayden in the line	
	27.x.17		2/Lt Shufford I.U. examined the B.O.S. the trench and garden on-nofles to clear during the canary went on the top & and the extent of connection available to take Company duty to extent Somme conversation Company in the line can Engineer Reserve extra relieved	
	28.x.17		Company in the line. 2/Lt HEATON was relieved by 2/Lt SHUFFREY 2/Lt GRUNDY remained Coy in ARIANE.	

Army Form C. 2118

WAR DIARY
or
INTELLIGENCE SUMMARY

(Erase heading not required.)

Instructions regarding War Diaries and Intelligence Summaries are contained in F. S. Regs., Part II. and the Staff Manual respectively. Title Pages will be prepared in manuscript.

Place	Date	Hour	Summary of Events and Information	Remarks and references to Appendices
	1/3/17		During the day enemy aircraft was actively active. All of our anti-aircraft guns kept them away. One enemy plane successfully dived on a rail waggon which descended in flames near ÉCURIE. The plane fired rockets to notify whereabouts of anti-aircraft shots were. It was active between 2 & 3 P.M. during which our anti-aircraft were active.	JMB
	2/3/17		Right sector gun relieved by 2 Fresh teams. Located in Right sector managed in hand to breech in carrying out operations. the following morning. After reported damaged by officer in charge. The shape experienced was new in character from an old German Dressing Station N.W. of BROOKES. Re-emplaced and on a slight a thick smoke being there on a concrete bed and the enemy managed to be heard of the enemy on the ER bed of a shown over ground matters. The Ten were houses in the old Dressing Stan.	JMB
	3/3/17		Company relieved from the line by the Nor-Northants. and line in case of duty 143 M.G. Coy. the relief was started at 10 P.M. was completed by 12-30 A.M. 14.F.C. Coy. are now 12 guns in the line having taken on a 2 Brigade front. A good day of officers was made. Deck deal of Officers decent/departs came into connection during the day in the South.	JMB

2449 Wt. W14957/Mgo 750,000 1/16 J.B.C. & A. Forms/C.2118/12.

Army Form C. 2118

WAR DIARY
or
INTELLIGENCE SUMMARY
(Erase heading not required.)

Instructions regarding War Diaries and Intelligence Summaries are contained in F. S. Regs., Part II. and the Staff Manual respectively. Title Pages will be prepared in manuscript.

Place	Date	Hour	Summary of Events and Information	Remarks and references to Appendices
	3/3/17		A preparer shaft and dug-out shaft, what was manned out by degrees at the workshop, 5 in number who also worked the Rai Sig Station. Two anti-aircraft MGs were also mounted. Early morning 2,300M site given the right of Bois and supplies to our Sa' RICHER Bench is being used from this place in connection with a plan made by one J.R. Hart the object of this was immediately for the removal of the existing forage.	P.C.B
	4/3/17		Company at rest in camp 56 near ELISIER	P.C.B
	5/3/17		Gear and Gun stores cleaned. Has storm caused Back contents of a bolsters. Pants were, our rifle gear were made fresh for the purpose of being the Bear Inventive for heavy work. There are done in date came	P.C.B
	6/3/17		Company parade for boots, gear and gun stores cleaned. Proof of bolsters carried on. New 8 degrees in MAG forage relief. Lieut J.C. Burtall, MC goes to Depot on MAG forage relief.	P.C.B

2449 Wt. W14957/M90 750,000 1/16 J.B.C. & A. Forms/C.2118/12.

Army Form C. 2118

WAR DIARY
or
INTELLIGENCE SUMMARY
(Erase heading not required.)

Instructions regarding War Diaries and Intelligence Summaries are contained in F.S. Regs., Part II. and the Staff Manual respectively. Title Pages will be prepared in manuscript.

Place	Date	Hour	Summary of Events and Information	Remarks and references to Appendices
	7/3/17	11.0 A.M.	Brigade Intelligence Officer Lieut. Nau Rev. delivered an address to officers and N.C.O's of all Coys. held in the Military Intelligence. Company moved into the line relieving 1st Bn R.M. playing 1 gun in the lines in Coy. to reserve post seen in BRIGADE RES. AREA, relief completed 12.30 A.M. 8/3/17. 6 men & 1 N.C.O. in one gun.	9
	8/3/17		Company in the line. Once received to reinforce the 1/6 R. Nav. R. holding the Right Sector of the Bde.	9
	9/3/17	2.0 A.M.	1/6 R. Nav. R. successfully raided German front line trench, capturing 2 enemy M.G's and 6 prisoners. Our seen in this Company operated to the advancing damage and the retirement of the raiding party. No casualties occurred.	9
	10/3/17		Company in the line. 110 h.m. 2 Hostile German in the Right Sector co-operated with artillery. No enemy raid followed.	9
	11/3/17		Company in the line. Men taken relief of the men engaged, so that the new men into the Right Sector of the Bde. above from this position which was considered unsuitable by the Reserve Sector. Relief was received	9
	12/3/17		enemy fire.
Company in the line.	9
	13/3/17		Company in the line. Bn. Rev. Peton relief, Left Sector (Branch) were relieved by Coys in RESERVE at Company Hqrs. Coy. in Bde. R.N.D. moved up into RESERVE (Company Hqrs.)	9

Army Form C. 2118.

WAR DIARY
or
INTELLIGENCE SUMMARY
(Erase heading not required.)

Instructions regarding War Diaries and Intelligence Summaries are contained in F.S. Regs., Part II. and the Staff Manual respectively. Title Pages will be prepared in manuscript.

Place	Date	Hour	Summary of Events and Information	Remarks and references to Appendices
	14/3/17		Company in the line.	
	15/3/17		Company in the line.	
	16/3/17		~~Battalion Headquarters.~~ C.O. attended conference at Bde Hdqrts. Receiving orders to co-operate with 143 Inf Bde in an attack on German line SOUTH EAST of the Gommecourt with the artillery support of the 143 Inf Bde was ordered to act and to attend. ZERO hour to be notified later. Received our objective. ZERO hour was fixed as 16 and 17 hours. The attack was to take place at 16 and 17 hours.	JCB
	17/3/17		12-midnight Officers and men in Company Hdqrs. in accordance with orders issued for attack. 1-30 A.M. 2 guns of S.A.A. Coy. and 4 guns of Hawks Coy. co-operated with the artillery barrage on the right of HAWKS COY. Men which were to the 1-30 A.M. 2 guns of the RIGHT SECTOR also fired. These 2 guns placed on the RIGHT SECTOR and continued firing until 2-15 A.M. & 2 Divisional ZERO not fired a barrage. 12 Divisional guns fired 15 minutes. 2-15 A.M. message received that attack was successful on Coy. 2-30 A.M. Sent down several things and information arrived with artillery fire at 3.30 A.M. Nobody then reported 143 Bde successful in their attack. 3-30 A.M. Forced our return to the trenches. 143 Inf Bde arms and kit were brought forward into the trenches for a release of the Bde men at the examining line for examination of men from 7/R Warwicks into our dumps of Germans taken through the German line with the 9/R Scottish 7/L SHUFFREY between these and the examining line with the Bde. Nine Lines ...	JCB

2449 Wt. W14957/M90 750,000 1/16 J.B.C. & A. Forms/C.2118/12.

WAR DIARY
or
INTELLIGENCE SUMMARY

(Erase heading not required.)

Army Form C. 2118

Place	Date	Hour	Summary of Events and Information	Remarks and references to Appendices
	17/3/17		At 2.0 PM. O.C. 143 M.G. Coy. having been notified of the situation gave orders for 2/Lt SHERREY and the period of a land of the 2nd INF.BDE which at this time extended from 2 WEST side of SOMME CANAL BANK at a point immediately south of PARGONNE, 500 yds S.W. this was now completed by 4.30 PM. Relieving the men in the line now consisting of either [illegible] up to [illegible] BRACHES and men were silent there tactically and took [illegible]. Intermittent enemy shelling during day.	GCH
	18/3/17		2/Lt SHERREY departed in his intelligence report when there was no activity in defence by speed of the front of the enemy [illegible] from BRIGADE founded to the line of the railway retirement of the enemy N.E. and EAST. LIEUT. J.C. BROMHILL M.C. theoretical the advanced positions of the 1/6 R. BN. R. on the N side of the SOMME, N.E. of PERONNE as far as four road 500 yds S. of ST DENIS. No enemy encounted with. 12 noon company moved out from POE to another to REST AREA near FRISE. This move was completed 10 PM.	GCH
	19/3/17		Company at rest. Guns and stores and men's clothing cleaned.	GCH
	20/3/17		Company at rest. Received French table cart made to work and company in transport used hutted and the land kept ventilated used own continual so this period definite housing was foreseen of the next report, and reducing number apparently on obtaining facility there remained as a security march and [illegible]	GCH

WAR DIARY
or
INTELLIGENCE SUMMARY

(Erase heading not required.)

Army Form C. 2118.

Instructions regarding War Diaries and Intelligence Summaries are contained in F. S. Regs., Part II. and the Staff Manual respectively. Title Pages will be prepared in manuscript.

Place	Date	Hour	Summary of Events and Information	Remarks and references to Appendices
	20/3/17		Owing to the Machine Officers being in PERONNE reconnoitring villages, we were not in action.	
	21/3/17	2	There was further talks at the H.Q. orders to proceed to reconnoitre positions. 2/Lt SPINK taken ill & length of company during his absence was reduced but we balance of men and guns the company was unfit for action.	
	22/3/17		Company went in rest at AVONWOOD. Right throughout day received the twenty Lewis Gun withdrawn from out of company of Infantry gun of all that the Division were to give up with two Civilians of Home - E gun. C.S.M. THOMSON, C.Q.M.S. BROWN and 62 O.R. were Attached. 2/Lt NORRIS. A new Engine with new wheels was found. Lt. G. T. THOMAS took over duties of Adjt. 2/Lt INSKIPP took over temporary command of "A" Section. 2/Lt SPINK posted to "A" Section.	
	23/3/17	26	O.C. 143 M.G. Coy received orders 12 noon to send a little party to PERONNE immediately. 2/Lt NORRIS and 3 signallers and 2 men of details sent under orders received into the company to proceed to PERONNE. Company was ready to move off 2 P.M. complete with Transport. Conditional was killed by 7:30 P.M. Completable shells were then prepared from rear of trench.	

Army Form C. 2118.

WAR DIARY
or
INTELLIGENCE SUMMARY.
(Erase heading not required.)

Place	Date	Hour	Summary of Events and Information	Remarks and references to Appendices
	24/3/17		2nd O.C. 143 M.G. Coy. reported that they were with the B.M. on reconnaissance around front line and way to Brigade observation at BRUENCOURT. Patrol from "A" Coy at BRUENCOURT. The right of the 142s on heavy point and met by line 2nd Battn. Pte NORRIS, MAY and HEATON were 2pm were killed when moving out of position to support infantry line. No flares and were not met by heavy fire. Confirmed high - and engaged by machine gun & infantry fire.	[signature]
BRUENCOURT	25/3/17		All now at Officers' Mess from left PERONNE to company Hqrs at BRUENCOURT 9 AM. Reconnaissance of PERONNE area made & reported completed by midday. Reconnaissance of Company Hqrs BRUENCOURT WOOD the Inspector 2pm area ok by 2/Lt SPINK was made and is on report. 2/Lt JAMES returned 2/Lt NORRIS in the instruction. MC. Capt. GRUNDY with Lieut. BRENNAN returned to G.S. Two employments for reduction of fallen TH 51.77. 7 II a 481, 6091, K.1a.30, T.14.6.77, T.U.26, B.21 0.290 21 (approx.) were relieved or entering and fighting killed & Batn. moved back to Divisional Reserve at BRUNCOURT. Some casualties. No casualties.	[signature]

WAR DIARY
or
INTELLIGENCE SUMMARY

Army Form C. 2118.

Place	Date	Hour	Summary of Events and Information	Remarks and references to Appendices
	26/3/17		Company in the line. All quiet. 2/Lt Norris was posted at Jg.a.8.1. and took a patrol upon reported to the transport lines.	[signed]
	27/3/17	2. A.M.	Instructions were received for Company Headqrs to move from Jg.a.39 to BUSS WOOD J.11.a. 9.6. c.a.m. of J.9.a.39. Company Headquarters were established by vicinity of BUSS WOOD. The transport lines were now moved then PERONNE & BUIRE WOOD in the neighbourhood of J.16.a. This move was completed by 2.15 pm.	[signed]
			Again positions were established at the following places (shown). E.20 (Stations on high ground) D.24.b.4.4. E.26.d.55. E.25.d.90. 2/Lt HAYES with 2 sec. came into the line. 2/Lt NORRIS G/L PERONNE on leave to U.K. O.C. 11.0 PM O.C. 143 M.G. Coy. reconnoitred line from B.M. 143 INGRÉ. East of COMBLES & LONGUEVESNES. Telephone line to be completed to Company below west sector. Lt. HEATON to be relieved. 17 C. OFFICER. INFORMATION LEFT BN. 3/LT HEATON & RGT. BN. SGT. PHILLIPS took 2 guns from 2/LT INSKIP.	[signed]
	28/3/17	2. A.M.	A.M. Operation Order 128 was received. Company Headqrs & section and received orders to move to LONGUEVESNES. Move was carried out by Noon. Company Headquarters formed & Longuevesnes transport park was completed. 2 guns with Sgt. PHILLIPS in TINCOURT WOOD were withdrawn.	[signed]

WAR DIARY
or
INTELLIGENCE SUMMARY

Army Form C. 2118.

Place	Date	Hour	Summary of Events and Information	Remarks and references to Appendices
	28/3/17		Repairs of ranging guns at the Kilns took [?], E20c18, E20c central, E20a of 7.17. E20a47 E4a54 E27a26, and 2 guns at E10d 6. Ranging registration shoots and reference tests to lessen lowcousness. At 11.30am O.C. 142 M.G. Coy met 3" Corps M.G.O.	
	29/3/17		2/Lt May and JAMES went to reconnoitre [?] ridge 7/r SPINK west into the line. 2/Lt SPINK met. Preparation of guns ammn on the 29".	
	30/3/17		2/Lt HAYES and 2/Lt HEATON went to reconnoitre near the Road. 2/Lt 2 gun emplts. 2/Lt HAYES at SUNKEN RD. VILLIERS FAUCON were selected. Guns reconnoitre at an early of 8" stages at 2 gun teams 7/r SPINK and E20 a 28 were nullied and transferred to pointe E20a99 to replace 7/Lt HEATONs 2 teams in area E20. At 8-30 pm. O.C. 163 M.G Coy was stated of the 118. Inf. Bde. & Lt SHERREY was ordered in liaison offic. of the 118 Bde. at ERLEY. At 10-30 am O.C. 143 M.G Coy received orders to support the attack to be made by the 11" Infr. Bde. on PEZIERE. 8 gun teams in area E10a to gun coving a frontage of fire to support the rd. M6B06 and the stakes on EPHEY. Lt SHERREY 2/Lts May JAMES and HAYES	

Army Form C. 2118.

WAR DIARY
or
INTELLIGENCE SUMMARY.
(Erase heading not required.)

Instructions regarding War Diaries and Intelligence Summaries are contained in F. S. Regs., Part II. and the Staff Manual respectively. Title pages will be prepared in manuscript.

Place	Date	Hour	Summary of Events and Information	Remarks and references to Appendices
	3/5/17		Was in charge of Thos SCOTT O.C. reconnoitred and detailed the HDQRTS at E.10.a.2.6. LT BROMHALL M.C. was LIAISON OFFICER at BROMMALL. Rest of relief GRESSUSART WOOD to take over and and carried from GRESSUSART WOOD E.10.a.2.6. At 1-30 PM O.C. reconnoitred positions reported. At 7.30 PM O.C. 143 M.G Coy received orders that an attack would be made at dawn by the C.R. WARR on PEIZER. One gun under 2nd Lt MAY would advance with the L.I.S.T. Company of the BATTn. 3 guns under 2nd Lt HAIGH would withdraw will support Company and would be consolidation 4 guns under 2nd Lt SHUFFREY and 2nd Lt SPINK reserve at Rail Head GRESSBOSSART WOOD. All guns and ammunition to be drawn from the Depot by 2nd Lt INSKIPP in relation to liaison of the Right Regt by 2nd JAMES.	

Signed [signature] Capt,
Cmdg. 143rd M. G. Coy.

Vol 16.

WAR DIARY.

143rd Machine Gun Coy.

1st April — 30 April 1917.

Army Form C. 2118.

WAR DIARY
or
INTELLIGENCE SUMMARY.
(Erase heading not required.)

Instructions regarding War Diaries and Intelligence Summaries are contained in F. S. Regs., Part II. and the Staff Manual respectively. Title pages will be prepared in manuscript.

Place	Date	Hour	Summary of Events and Information	Remarks and references to Appendices
	1.4.17		At dawn 4 M.G. accompanied the 1/6 R.War.R. in their attack on PEZIERE 2/Lt HAY was in command of the left team attached to the left Coy. 2/Lt HAYES 2 gun team was with the support Coy and assisted in consolidation. Lieut SHUFFREY and 2/Lt SPINK were at Advanced Brigade H.dqrs with 16 Lewis. O.C. 148 M.G.Coy with Lieut BROMHALL M.C. were at advanced H.dqrs during these operations. At 12.5pm O.C. 148 M.G.Coy received instructions that 2/Lt QM Stone and Reserve Section were to move forward to SAULCOURT this move was completed by 4pm and the Coys were being used by incoming General Brigade SHUFFREY and 2/Lieut SPINK reported to Coy H.dqrs from Advanced Brigade H.dqrs. No casualties.	[signature]
	2.4.17.		2/Lieuts JAMES and HEATON relieved 2/Lieuts MAY and HAYES in the line. Coys in reserve were engaged on improving and reconnoitring trenches. No casualties. Coy transport moved from TINCOURT WOOD to SAULCOURT WOOD.	[signature]
	3.4.17.		Coy in the line. Reclining in reserve improving trenches. No casualties.	[signature]
	4.4.17.		Lieut SHUFFREY relieved 2/Lieut JAMES and HEATON in the line. 2/Lieut SPINK with 3 gun team relieved 4 gun team of the 148 M.G.Coy in the line. Coy received thanks of III Corps from Commander in Chief, Congratulations of G.O.C. 48 B. Div and his congratulations on the success of the operations. Jockey above the Advanced Coy with the Division Coy engaged in making wire or shelters for men in the line. 3.O.R. taken in attempt of Coy. No casualties.	[signature]

A5834 Wt. W4973/M687 750,000 8/16 D.D. & L. Ltd. Forms/C.2118/13.

WAR DIARY or INTELLIGENCE SUMMARY

Army Form C. 2118.

Instructions regarding War Diaries and Intelligence Summaries are contained in F.S. Regs., Part II. and the Staff Manual respectively. Title pages will be prepared in manuscript.

(Erase heading not required.)

Place	Date	Hour	Summary of Events and Information	Remarks and references to Appendices
	5/4/17		Company in the Corps Reserve. Sections conducted route & skill's for teams in the line. No casualties.	SAH
	6/4/17		2/Lt Inskipp and May relieved Lt Surridge and 2/Lt Spink. Period of consolidation was resumed. Range of fire shifted from 920 m 80 m 100 m. Division and G.O.C. Division and G.S.O.C. Division O.C. 143 M.G.Coy congratulated Company Officers N.C.Os and men on their conduct during the operations and effort in general. One N.C.O. was Pte — (wounded) for their recent event.	SAH
	7/4/17		Capt Grundy left for leave to U.K. Lt Bromhall M.C. took over command of Company. 2/Lt Jones and Hayes marched to the line to commence	SAH
	8/4/17		2/Lt Heaton and Spink relieved 2/Lt Mar and Inskipp from the line and arrived in our area. No casualties.	SAH
	9/4/17		O.O. 133 was received by the O.C. 143 Machine Gun Coy that the Company moved to relieve 1 Bde 125 M.G.Coy. Company orders for the relief on the night of 9/10th April were issued. 9 N.C.Os of the 125 M.G.Coy moved to Longavesnes. No casualties.	SAH
	10/4/17		The 143 M.G.Coy was relieved in the line by the 125 M.G.Coy. 2/Lts Heaton and Spink remained in line with the 125 M.G.Coy. 2/Lt Bromhall M.C. conducted O.C. 125 M.G.C. around to all Gun positions. Coy Hqrs, Q.M. stores, Reserve gun teams moved from Saulcourt to Longavesnes. 2 M.G.s & other kit were collected on the Corps lorries and	SAH

A.5834. Wt. W4973/M687 750,000 8/16 D.D. & L. Ltd. Forms/C.2118/13.

Army Form C. 2118.

WAR DIARY
or
INTELLIGENCE SUMMARY.
(Erase heading not required.)

Place	Date	Hour	Summary of Events and Information	Remarks and references to Appendices
	10/4/17		Returned over to the 125 M.G. Coy. All ranks 57 C SE were marched over. Pl. with no horses available to Bob Hoors. A report was sent to Bob Hoors to obtain plate of mules taken over in LONGAVESNES.	[initials]
	11/4/17		The whole of the company moved from LONGAVESNES to billets in PERONNE. There was a inspected our pl.t.e. to Bob Hoors. 4/s HENTON and SPINK sent out of the line and proceeded to PERONNE.	[initials]
	12/4/17		Company in reserve at PERONNE. Day was devoted to fairly easy exercises and fitting them with new clothes.	[initials]
	13/4/17		Company in reserve at PERONNE. Day was devoted to cleaning guns, gun shoes & equipment. Pte. authorisation 27589 "Pte BATCHELOR.W." was sentenced to 10 days F.P.No.1 for "slothful conduct" by not being ready in time.	[initials]
	14/3/17		Company in reserve in PERONNE. Parade were held. Received orders Cof S. and R. E. Limbers were packed. Lt. BROMWELL.M.C. as O.C. took in a place assent of the operation of the northern axis of force on 16/4/17 to 17/4/17 as the 143 Inf. Bde B.O. S.P. 7213) Pte ALCOCK.H.E. was returned to S.P.F.P.No.1. for completing with order and pt. 126 Inf. Bde to parade D.O. 1135 was relief of the OC 143 M.G.A.y	[initials]

WAR DIARY
or
INTELLIGENCE SUMMARY

Army Form C. 2118.

Place	Date	Hour	Summary of Events and Information	Remarks and references to Appendices
	14/4/17		Operation Orders for the Relief were issued. O.C. 143 M.G. Coy established O.C. 125 M.G. Coy at SAUCOURT.	
	15/4/17		Company Heights, Pistols and Transport moved from PERONNE to SAUCOURT now on reported at Place by 12-45 P.M. At 4 P.M. 2/Lt SWIFFREY and 2/Lt JAMES with 3 Sgts came out and 3 Gun teams of the 125 Inf Bde M.G. Coy to the Right Sec. Coy. 9/Lt. Inskip and 2nd Sgt went to Peronne and received 9 teams Relief of Gun teams of the 143 Inf Bde M.G. Coy was completed by 12-45 P.M. Left Sec. Coy Relief not reported complete by 12-45 P.M. Guns and ammunition and stores were at Company HQRS at 5.a. 59. Received Guns and teams in SAUCOURT WOOD (East) [illegible] Guns in SAUCOURT WOOD (West). 2/Lt SWIFFREY and 2/Lt INSKIP reconnoitred ground in rear of the sector prior to Relief.	
	16/4/17	At 1.0 P.M.	O.C. 143 M.G. Coy received O.O. 135 stop the 165 Inf Bde advance to fine from [illegible] stop 3 Sect South of 2.6 PRISELFM CATELET COPSE stops to the new [illegible] X22.d.99 to X22.a.35 [illegible] to X22.a.17. X22.b.22.d.99 the right 16/17 inst. 8 Guns to be taken to position on new line of Coy H.Q.'s Relief to [illegible] all Guns reach 2nd positions by following of Orders Guns remain at camp in SAUCOURT till JAMES able to [illegible] Guns Right Battalion [illegible] INSKIP at [illegible]	

WAR DIARY
or
INTELLIGENCE SUMMARY

Army Form C. 2118.

Place	Date	Hour	Summary of Events and Information	Remarks and references to Appendices
	16/4/17	6.30	Battalion relieved the Left Battalion B. Coy under 2/Lt Hayes relieved the Right Sector. H Coy under 2/Lt May in reserve in the Left Sector. Coy Headqrs all accounted at C.29.59. Company accounted together with O.C. E.6.O.8.9.10.C.M.J M.G. Coy reinforced by 10 guns over and above the Coy having the normal equipment of his guns and 1 O.R. in Reserve and S.O.S. rockets and 2/Lt Noring returning from leave E.O.K.	(signature)
	17/4/17	2.0 a.m.	2/Lt Heaton proceeded to advanced Coy Hdqrs. 2/Lt Heaton went into the line with his men. 2/Lt Insurmo relieved 2/Lt Spink with 15 Coy Hdqrs. 2/Lt Norris went into the line. 2/Lt James relieved O.C. much day 0.0.137. Dispositions: A Coy 143/Hdqrs Well defined after some to the line with Right Barr East of the Brown Line No 2 in the Outpost and 2/Lt Support to meet Left Battn East of the Brown Line. 3 in outpost and 2 in Reserve and 2 in reserve to Coy Hdqrts in the Brown Line came in sometime reserve of Coy Hdqrts. Company Hdqrts moved to Peiziere by Wood 68 as per O.O.137 O.R's covering guns and Easy on Lichen I.O.R. available. The platoon. Reserves and fields made more in Peiziere to Company.	(signature)

HDQRTS. O.C RESERVE BATTN.

WAR DIARY or INTELLIGENCE SUMMARY

Army Form C. 2118.

Place	Date	Hour	Summary of Events and Information	Remarks and references to Appendices
	18/4/17		Wire was sent to Brigade at 5 P.M. 137 giving the dispositions of the Guns together with Bar as follows:- RIGHT BATTN. OUTPOST LINE. F5a 2095 and X25 central. SUPPORT GUNS F4a 2570 and X27 b04. LEFT BATTN. OUTPOST. GUNS X22 074 and X22 c09. SUPPORT GUNS X21 c65 and X21 a15. BROWN LINE GUNS. F20 32 by day, the gun is at F20 c72 at night, remaining gun at B1 b73, X25 a73, X25 a 3). 4 Guns in RESERVE at Company HQrs at W30 c 67. 2/Lt SPINK relieved Lt SHUFFREY. Lt THOMAS as ADJT and 2/Lt BLAKE as I. Officer were trepans at the burial service by Army Chaplain of the 6' R. Wa. R. of 3/Lt Inskipp D. at SAULCOURT. O.C. 143 M.G. Coy consulted the O.C. 126 M.G. Coy round the line. 143 Lt T.C. BROMHALL M.C. name was sent to Bde HQrts for a lecture at Army Schools on tactical use of Machine Gun in connection with infantry. No casualties.	[signature]

WAR DIARY
or
INTELLIGENCE SUMMARY.
(Erase heading not required.)

Army Form C. 2118.

Place	Date	Hour	Summary of Events and Information	Remarks and references to Appendices
	19/4/17		Company in the line. Dispositions of the Coys were as follows:- RIGHT BTN. X 29 c 20, X 25 c 45.00; X27 c 90, X27 c 72, LEFT BTN X 21 c 75, X 22 c 84, X 22 a 18, X 21 c 15.85. BROWN LINE GUNS, RIGHT F 2 c 72, F 1 c 70, LEFT X 25 a 73, X 25 a 37. 4 in Reserve Coy HdQrts W 30 c 68. 2 Officers, 10 O.R. of 156 M.G. Coy were sent to the line for instruction. No casualties.	
	20/4/17	9.30 P.M.	O.C. 153 M.G. Coy received O.O. 138. 143. 2/Lt Bell relieved by 126 2/Lt Bell in the line. In the night of the 20/21 Companys after relief moved to Rose Hills as follows:- LONGAVESNES. Company Operation orders were issued by O.C. 153 M.G. Coy. 2/Lt Hayes was relieved in the line by 2/Lt Sumner, 2/Lt May and Norris were relieved in the line by 2/Lt JAMES and HENTON. 10 casualties.	
	21/4/17	12.0 Midnight	Centers Kits, R.A. Stores, Transport lines moved to Longavesnes dusring the afternoon. Coys in the evening relieved by 126 M.G. Coy after tea. Relief was reported complete to Bde Hdqrts. 12.0 Midnight to concentrate.	

Army Form C. 2118.

WAR DIARY
or
INTELLIGENCE SUMMARY.
(Erase heading not required.)

Instructions regarding War Diaries and Intelligence Summaries are contained in F. S. Regs., Part II. and the Staff Manual respectively. Title pages will be prepared in manuscript.

Place	Date	Hour	Summary of Events and Information	Remarks and references to Appendices
	22/4/17		Capt. Col O'Gornely returned from leave and assumed command of the Company. Working parties on LONGAVESNES spur in open about and digging and improving huts.	[initials]
	23/4/17		Company in huts LONGAVESNES. Day one of cleaning sec guns about & e. Lt Thompson and 1 Cos Corporal in charge of party in salvage work. Lieut. Drummond 340110 26 Dudley. J. appointed as acting F.P. No.1.	[initials]
	24/4/17		Company at rest LONGAVESNES. Day one of cleaning and testing Lewes, Ry mounts and to company, 3 ettergers 3 mules and 1 L.D. good condition. Orders received from Brigade for company to assemble at VILLERS-FAUCON in Divisional Reserve 4.15 AM 25th inst. Bate order arrived 11.0 PM	[initials]
	25/4/17		Company less O.M Stores loaded for the line 2.45 AM and after reported to Bde in position VILLERS-FAUCON at 4-5 AM. 8.0 - 10-30 AM Bde order to dump too transport and hutted 7.45 AM. Order received to dump too transport new hutted at VILLERS-FAUCON Company returned to LONGAVESNES and rested during remainder of day.	[initials]

WAR DIARY
or
INTELLIGENCE SUMMARY.
(Erase heading not required.)

Army Form C. 2118.

Instructions regarding War Diaries and Intelligence Summaries are contained in F.S. Regs., Part II. and the Staff Manual respectively. Title pages will be prepared in manuscript.

Place	Date	Hour	Summary of Events and Information	Remarks and references to Appendices
	26/4/17		Company in reserve at LONGAVESNES. Trench-digging and telephoning was carried out. During the afternoon heavy rain fell, neither the company work completed.	
	27/4/17		Company in reserve at LONGAVESNES. General parade. G.O. N.C.O. arms officer and cooks charges. Parade. During the afternoon the final of the facing competition was conducted. Brig.Gen. Commanding 163. Inf. Bde. was present to greet and present Bde. Major and some very interesting talks were read.	
	28/4/17		Company in reserve at LONGAVESNES. Gun drill and foot drill and Lewis Gun classes were carried on. O.O.140 received by the O.C. 163 M.G.Coy. at 9.30 p.m. that the Company would move out billets at PERONNE on 29" inst.	
	29/4/17		O.O. for moving into billets at PERONNE was issued by O.C. 163 M.G.Coy. 16 Company complete with O/H.V.L. mules, moved into billets at PERONNE. Move was reported complete to Bde HQ.RTS by O.O. 141 at 5.30 p.m. 12 mules with B.O. 141 were received. Company march now to ECLUSIER.	

Army Form C. 2118.

WAR DIARY
or
INTELLIGENCE SUMMARY.
(Erase heading not required.)

Instructions regarding War Diaries and Intelligence Summaries are contained in F. S. Regs., Part II. and the Staff Manual respectively. Title pages will be prepared in manuscript.

Place	Date	Hour	Summary of Events and Information	Remarks and references to Appendices
	30/4/17		March and entrained as per C.O. 141, 00 & any coys arr. Nice to entrain FRISE, Nr. Péronne. Train total 62C, 1,000 G.II. 26. Horse reported complete 2.0 p.m. Remainder of day employed unloading and stowing kits.	[signature]
			See ref. reference to place during the next days incl. to place on France sheet 62°, 62 N.E. and 57° S.E.	[signature]

for [signature] Capt.
Cmdg. 143rd M. G. Coy.

SECRET

War Diary.

143rd Machine Gun Company.

1st May. 1917.   to   31st May. 1917.

Army Form C. 2118.

WAR DIARY
or
INTELLIGENCE SUMMARY.
(Erase heading not required.)

Instructions regarding War Diaries and Intelligence Summaries are contained in F.S. Regs., Part II. and the Staff Manual respectively. Title pages will be prepared in manuscript.

Place	Date	Hour	Summary of Events and Information	Remarks and references to Appendices
	1/5/17		Box in rest at FRISE. The day was spent in cleaning guns and rifles. Afternoon devoted to sport.	[initials]
	2/5/17		Box in rest. Parades Cams drill until 11 A.M. officers mounted the ground. Rest of afternoon until 4 p.m. SPN n+ N.C.O. to buy anything there might be required by the men. Coy drill between 5 & 6 pm. Box 40 Box 10 was inspected by C.O. all Box had worn and rifles at PERONNE. Coy Orders were issued.	[initials]
	3/5/17		Box in rest. Bn HQ at FRISE. No reports received as yet. Remainder of day spent in cleaning and in moving kits.	[initials]
	4/5/17		Box in rest at PERONNE. Parades - Physical Muster - Platoon drill, bayonet and gun cleaning.	[initials]
	5/5/17		Box in rest at PERONNE. Box at drill also fatigue parties sent from each section for a coy muster parade. 8 guns went to the R.E. Dump to be exchanged for new ones. O.C. No 3 & No 4 Coy reconnoitred and reported on proposed Outposts. Troops marched at 3.0 p.m.	[initials]
	6/5/17		Box in rest at PERONNE. Brigade church parade for all denominations during the afternoon, company stand by under Brig. Comdr. before tea.	[initials]

WAR DIARY
or
INTELLIGENCE SUMMARY

Army Form C. 2118.

Place	Date	Hour	Summary of Events and Information	Remarks and references to Appendices
	7/5/17		Company in rest at PERONNE. Bath parade and arms and equip. insp. and fatigue duties. During the afternoon sports.	
	8/5/17		Company in rest at PERONNE. Coy. to clean and inspect rifles, web equipment & box respirators. Platoon in training. Note hours for work out. During the afternoon O.C. 143 M.G. Coy. spoke on efficient use of rifle. Proved fatal on various hits from F.85.	
	9/5/17		Company in rest at PERONNE. Squad and Company drill instruction in range & musketry and fast aircraft drill. During the afternoon sports.	
	10/5/17		Company in rest at PERONNE. Parade was squad and company drill firing and immediate action.	
	11/5/17		Company in rest at PERONNE. Parade was squad drill physical training new battle drill and Lewis gun. Battle gear ready to move. 6.30 pm O.C. 143 M.G. Coy. received G.O. 143. Coy. confirmed orders move in the early morning from PERONNE to LE MESNIL area.	

Captain Machine Gun Officer

A5834 Wt. W.4973/M687 750,000 8/16 D. D. & L. Ltd. Forms/C.2118/13.

WAR DIARY
or
INTELLIGENCE SUMMARY

Army Form C. 2118.

Place	Date	Hour	Summary of Events and Information	Remarks and references to Appendices
	12/5/17		Company moved according to Batl. Order age O.O.1443. Arrived in camping area LE MESNIL Ref. USC 38 at 11.15 AM during the afternoon OC 143 MGC and Lt BROMHALL MC visited HQrs of the M.G.C. in the line. At 9.0 PM OC 143 MGC received OO 144 company moved to FRENICOURT and that the Batl also moved. At Bn MGC during the night 13/14th moved to Cotes wire reached companies operations.	
	13/5/17		Company moved to FRENICOURT as in OO 1444. 2nd 143 Inf Bde 2nd Corps MG Coy moved to the 5th Army area and then H. Corps to XV Corps. Coy arty left and met with GOC XV Corps. Coy arty arrived FRENICOURT 11.0 AM Coy OO 141 was ordered to the OO 1444 Coy arty 44 Bde took on hut and Lt SMICKERS during afternoon gave orders to Lt BROWN at Chapel Hoors confry HQrs at 112 t 35 Ref. France 57CNW. GM Mores and Humphreys ant twelve officers and men teams of FRENICOURT.	
	14/5/17	11.0 AM	Coy to be at the Lt Relief of the 34 MG Coy reported complete 11.0 AM. No casualties OC 143 MGC and Lt BROMHALL MC visited at Bn in afternoon and made out a now order. No exist set OR Watson Supervised Infantry Material position and demolished out.	

Army Form C. 2118.

WAR DIARY
or
INTELLIGENCE SUMMARY
(Erase heading not required.)

Instructions regarding War Diaries and Intelligence Summaries are contained in F. S. Regs., Part II. and the Staff Manual respectively. Title Pages will be prepared in manuscript.

Place	Date	Hour	Summary of Events and Information	Remarks and references to Appendices
	15/5/17		Company in the line. Situation very quiet. Lieut THOMAS with Coy. Cmd. sent back sick. Gun to casualties.	MSS
	16/5/17		Company in the line. Situation quiet. No casualties.	MSS
	17/5/17		Company in the line. 2nd Lt NORRIS relieved LIEUT SHUFFREY in the field. RESERVE Officers improving billets at MONCHIEL. No casualties.	MSS
	18.5.17		Company in the line. 2/Lt Jones relieved Lieut SHUFFREY in the line. Lt THOMAS returned to SA with sickness. Situation quiet. No casualties.	MSS
	19/5/17		Company in the line. Situation quiet.	MSS
	20/5/17		Company in the line. Situation quiet. Prisoner relieved 7/Lt HAYES in ext. line.	MSS
	21/5/17		Company were relieved by the 1/4th MG Coy in the line. The 2nd MG Coy took over 8 guns in the Divisional Reserve line. Company moved to FRENCHCOURT.	MSS
	22/5/17		Relief reported complete 11-0AM. Company at rest.	MSS
	23/5/17		Company at rest. Re-organising.	MSS
	24/5/17		Company at rest. Training - Physical training and musketry. MG Drill etc.	MSS

WAR DIARY or INTELLIGENCE SUMMARY

Army Form C. 2118.

Place	Date	Hour	Summary of Events and Information	Remarks and references to Appendices
	25/5/17		Company in rest. Physical training, especially drill, musketry, and immediate action.	MWD
	26/5/17		Company in rest. Having knee [tactical] scheme. Up applying on infantry attack and overhead firing. Method of carrying into action various kinds of ammunition, coys.	MWD
	27/5/17		Company in rest. Range firing. Judging distances, indication of targets, fire orders.	MWD
	28/5/17		Company in rest. Preparing for line.	MWD
	29/5/17		Company relieved 144 M.G.Coy in the line [at?] 9.35 a.m. 144 M.G.Coy relieved 8 guns in forward positions in the line. 1 officer, 30 casualties.	MWD
	30/5/17		Relief completed 10 A.M.	MWD
	31/5/17		Company in the line. Stoke my guns to character.	MWD

H.A. [Signature]
Capt.
Cmdg. 143rd M. G. Coy.

Confidential

War Diary

143rd Machine Gun Coy.

1st June 1917 — 30th June

Army Form C. 2118.

WAR DIARY
or
INTELLIGENCE SUMMARY.
(Erase heading not required.)

Instructions regarding War Diaries and Intelligence Summaries are contained in F. S. Regs., Part II. and the Staff Manual respectively. Title pages will be prepared in manuscript.

Place	Date	Hour	Summary of Events and Information	Remarks and references to Appendices
Nithful	1/6/17		Company in the line. Situation very quiet. Inter-section relief took place during the evening. No casualties.	
	2/6/17		Company in the line. Situation quiet. 1 O.R. wounded in scheme.	
	3/6/17		Company in the line. Situation normal. No casualties.	
	4/6/17		Company in the line. Situation normal. No casualties.	
	5/6/17		Company in the line. Situation normal. No casualties.	
	6/6/17		Company relief took place 1444-1146067 relieving 143 2/8 Coy in the line on the night 6/7 June. Situation Quiet. No casualties.	
	7/6/17		Relief reported complete 3.0 AM. 8 teams in Divisional Reserve. Rail remainder in rest.	
	8/6/17		Company in rest. Training and cleaning.	
	9/6/17		Company in rest. Training and range work.	
	10.6.17		Capt. R. G. BRONSHILL M.C. returned from Carter's Force with 20 R. & 2/Lt. JAMES. 9 Runners returned to Div Reserve 7 mm handed to Bgy. in rest. 2/Lt. JAMES skimmed tram leave struck with 15 Arrests. Violent thunderstorm during practice.	
	11.6.17		@ 2/Lt Thomas & B section relieved 4 teams in Div Res LEFT SECTOR. D Section C Section in the Right Sector Div. Res. Line. 3/Lt SPINK returned from D R Line to Batoon.	
	12.6.17		'A' 16 Section rested. B Guns in DR Line, remainder of Coy in rest. S.D. attacked Rifle Grenades fired	
	13.6.17		No. R. 3 Gun L. of BEAUNETZ heavily shelled during the day, moved to 18 yards father (having a mile) up to within 18 yds of the previous emplacement, afterwards aided by Coy Sergt-Major. Gun mounted. B.d.I. ventured special attention & firing Support Line & Front Line.	

WAR DIARY
or
INTELLIGENCE SUMMARY

(Erase heading not required.)

Army Form C. 2118.

Place	Date	Hour	Summary of Events and Information	Remarks and references to Appendices
	13.6.17		Each gun of the Coy represented 2 guns. 3 Batteries attacked, 1 Batto in Reserve. 2 guns from each Section were ordered to move with the 3rd wave of the attacking Battns, 2 guns from each Section were to give covering fire during the attack. One Section held in Reserve. The attack commenced at 8.30 am & proceeded at 10.30 am. Difficulties encountered were supply of ammunition & transport of guns during Overland line into its new position which would have been rendered shorter.	90.13
	14.6.17		C.O. attended Bde Conference. R/6pl THISTLETHWAITE & Pte ROBINSON went on leave to U.K. The Coy relieved the 143 Coy in the line in the RIGHT SECTOR. "B" SECTION relieving at GRAS & "B" Section in D.R. Line relieving 2 guns. 2/Lt MAY & PINN reconnoitred positions for barrage fire in area S.W. of FRONVILLE. 2/Lt SHUPPEREY 1/7th HEATON went into the FRONT LINE. 40 OR's arrived as reinforcements	90.13
	15.6.17		Coy relieved 143 M.G. Coy. 4 guns in support line by guns which had been in Right Sector. 2/Lt SPINN in charge of 8 guns of 4 guns 2/Lt JAMES relieved 2/Lt HEATON returned to Coy H.Q. 1/2nd Coy relieved to guns in Right D.R. line that Section moved in Reserve to Pte Bde H.Qrs. 2/Lt MAY reconed barrage. Relief completed 6.30 am 16th. 05:135 M.G. Coy assumed command of M.G. defences of Ronville.	90.13
	16.6.17		Coy in the line. Enemy extremely inactive. Pte Weston went on leave to U.K.	90.13
	17.6.17		Coy in the line. C.O. visited the 16th & 17th R.W.R. it Capts to make arrangements for forming Mills by the 1/6 R.W.R. on enemy post between these lines. 6 emplacements were ordered for 6 P.B. guns to put a burst barrage beyond the post to be raided.	90.13
	18.6.17		8 guns in the line with 10 guns. 6 guns in Reserve were moved up into positions for the barrage arranged at BOURSIES in Sunken after approaching difficulty which ended at X road NEW DOIGNIES. Pack to be used was S.M. road (AMBRA). 1800 yds E of BOURSIES, & from were in a line the SUNKEN ROAD running N.E. of L. mile of BOURSIES. 2 guns where low & from N.E of BOURSIES westerly. Right guns under command of 2/Lt MAY, 2 centre guns in command of 2/Lt HEATON, 2 L.H guns under command of 2/Lt WYATTS. Creep Barrage of Artillery & M.G.'s commenced at 11 pm. Raid was successful. Prisoners taken, 1 Officer & 49 O.R's	90.13

2449 Wt. W14957/M90 750,000 1/16 J.B.C. & A. Forms/C.2119/12.

Army Form C. 2118.

WAR DIARY
or
INTELLIGENCE SUMMARY.
(Erase heading not required.)

Instructions regarding War Diaries and Intelligence Summaries are contained in F.S. Regs., Part II and the Staff Manual respectively. Title pages will be prepared in manuscript.

Place	Date	Hour	Summary of Events and Information	Remarks and references to Appendices
	18.6.17		Heavy cannonade caused to the enemy. Guns were withdrawn by daylight on morning 19.19.17. 2/Lt BATCHELOR 1/8th War. R.	9.13
	19.6.17		Day in the line. Reserve gun teams making M.G. emplacements for tucking up and clearing up and etc. 2/Lt BATCHELOR 1/8 War. R. to arrange M.G. support for tucking operation if required. 6.13.21 inst.	9.13
	20.6.17		Day in the line. 2.0. 21st May, 2/Lt HEATON took up guns. 2.0 went to positions on the high ground LAGNICOURT - LOUVERVAL - MORCHIES. The object of these guns being to augment fire power of the N.E. of PRONVILLE. Left gun barrage SW. from PRONVILLE. Artillery emplacements went first and barrage time, brought up with the N roads to meet two schemes intended to isolate these positions with the front of the N road between the HINDENBURG line. S of PRONVILLE on the HINDENBURG line. 2/Lt HAYES relfd DEAN went on leave.	9.13
	21.6.17		Coy in the line 6 guns moved up into positions shown on the 20th inst. 2 guns of D Section on the RIGHT under 2/Lt MAY, 2 guns D Section under 2/Lt HEATON in centre. 2 guns on LEFT - Sgt. WATTS. All guns were searching and traffic into 12 ground and LEFT fired 16 Boches Bells of 1000 SAA from calls on positions at midnight. Total 8000 Rounds	9.13
	22.6.17		at 1 AM. Zero hour. Artillery and OR 6.5 opened fire for ½ hour on 2.15 am. All artillery died down to 2.30 AM. Fire stopped. 2.45 AM.G.S. placed in position. Worked up and laid guns on its limbers which had been left by in a dip behind the tank. Right gun 9 on the road in a cutting No 15. 2 Left gun 13. Day Left tank limbers and tanks had returned to their position in company. Day fire duration to pack saddle was moved close to brigade HQ. Guns & ammunition to their artillery positions - Company relieved by 144 M.G. Coy with the remainder.	9.13
	23.6.17	12.30 AM	Relief of the Company from the support line of the occupation of 8 guns position in 18 DIVISIONAL RES. Line were refd by completing the relief was executed in 2½ hours. No casualties. Company moved back to rest at HARLINCOURT. Guns & ammo under 2/Lt MAY & 2/Lt HEATON. Raid on PRONVILLE night unable to proceed.	9.13

A 2092. Wt. W18839/M1292 750,000. 1/17. D.D.&L., Ltd. Forms/C2118/12.

WAR DIARY
or
INTELLIGENCE SUMMARY.
(Erase heading not required.)

Army Form C. 2118.

Instructions regarding War Diaries and Intelligence Summaries are contained in F.S. Regs., Part II. and the Staff Manual respectively. Title pages will be prepared in manuscript.

Place	Date	Hour	Summary of Events and Information	Remarks and references to Appendices
	24.6.17		Company (½ A, ½ B, and C section) ad. Arat & Gunn in Div. Res. Line. O.C. Fisher ½ Coy. R.M.R.R. Sgt. Dale to Signallers course	9.6.B
	25.6.17		Company Training Programme Firing on Range carried out owing to insufficient officers being given in Section Officers 16 Men Section Transport etc. O.C. selected Officers to command at 5 p.m. Course of section leaders started Subjects: Raids, Patrols, Honours, Defence, Patrols Thrusts (Colonel) S.O. co M.B. section Company.	9.6.B
	26.6.17		Company Training Programme Party in ''''Carrying Party was Courses not owing 5-15 ½ Coy R.M.R.R. Practicing an attack which outlagged the Range — Gun drill — Reinforcements lately arrived first relieved to be moved 4 O.R. of Thanks received from Col. Hanson ½ R.M.R. for M.G. help rendered Section in the line ± Div. Res Line. Relieved by 2/Lt. James and 2/Lt. Spurr with C Sec. ''A'' Section. On Rifle Range and arrived	9.6.B
	27.6.17		Company Training Teams relieved 26/27 meeting and Company eg. Remainder of section camps 2/Lt. Thomas Sgt. Ruddis Sgt. Marriott has been to Amiens on duty ''B'' Section Revolver Shooting. Semi-Final Football Cup played Coy. Defeated by 5 men	9.6.B
	28.6.17		Company Training. Gas Drill – Revolver Revolver March. Knife Knife fighting Corps M.G.O. reported. Issued the Lewis Gas drill with the C.O. 2/Lt. Sheppard returned from 6.10 Day Leave + disb. of Bullets and Ammo. Lectures by Section Officers. Inspection by 2/Lt. of Transport arranged.	9.6.B
	29.6.17		Company training Saluting drill: gun drill: inspection of Lewis Gun by C.O.	Coy
	30.6.17		2/Lt. Thomas proceeded to Cahiers – G.H.Q. small arm school M.G. Mount. Coy moved to dinners near Gomiécourt. Coy still remaining in Du Six Rutbert Capt Coy 1/5 R.M.R.	Coy

WAR DIARY

143rd MACHINE GUN COY

1st July 1917 — 31st July 1917.

Army Form C. 2118.

WAR DIARY
or
INTELLIGENCE SUMMARY.
(Erase heading not required.)

Instructions regarding War Diaries and Intelligence Summaries are contained in F. S. Regs., Part II. and the Staff Manual respectively. Title pages will be prepared in manuscript.

Place	Date	Hour	Summary of Events and Information	Remarks and references to Appendices
GOMMECOURT	1.7.17		Coy in rest at GOMMECOURT	
	2.7.17		Coy in rest at GOMMECOURT	
	3.7.17		Detachment on the Div. Rest line relieved by the 76 M.G. Coy. Relief complete in turn marched to HAPLINCOURT	
BIENVILLERS	4.7.17		Coy paraded 9.0 G Div Staff Rode Attacking Scheme Detachment marched to Coy at BIENVILLERS	
	5.3.17		Brigade Tactical Scheme M.Gs gave covering of fire	
	6.7.17		10 men attacked from the north of the Role.	
	7.7.17		Company "standing by" for movement	
	8.7.17		Coy found standing by to Counterattack at BEAUMETZ-by-LOGES All limbered carts to be kept attached whilst caught. The town owing to the circumstances being of the east of the town. Time taken 1½ hours.	
	9.7.17		Coy paraded at ST OMER 1½ hrs distance in 20 minutes marched to billets at TILQUES of RESQUES	
	10.7.17		Officers and N.C.Os watched the training ground of 1 Div South Div. Company cleaning up	
	11.7.17		Coy at TILQUES "A" + "B" Sections practising movement in to position for tornado attack. "C" + "D" Sections similarly	
	12.7.17		Coy at TILQUES "C" + "D" Sections practising movement into position for barrage schemes LTC BROWNALL MC wished to join 58 M.G. Coy in 66 k WAY. detailed 2½ Coy 1+3 PM of Coy Memo attaching achieved arrived from Corps No 90.	
	13.7.17		O.E attended the South Div Pastern attack Coy at TILQUES. Infantry drill, cleaning of guns, etc.	
	14.7.17		Coy training at TILQUES	
	15.7.17		Coy Church parade	
	16.7.17		Coy Tactical Scheme by "A" + "B" Sections	
	17.7.17		Coy Tactical Scheme by "C" + "D" Sections LT DAVY taken on strength as 2/L	

Army Form C.2118.

WAR DIARY
or
INTELLIGENCE SUMMARY.
(Erase heading not required.)

Instructions regarding War Diaries and Intelligence Summaries are contained in F.S. Regs., Part II. and the Staff Manual respectively. Title pages will be prepared in manuscript.

Place	Date	Hour	Summary of Events and Information	Remarks and references to Appendices
	19.7.17		Coy in training. Coy photographed	
	21.7.17		2/Lt. Ic Bromhall to 2/Lt. Leys took command of 15 + MG. Coy	
	20.7.17		Coy sports. Fridge hatch shot by 2/Lt J. Willatt	
	21.7.17		Coy transport moved with 118 Inf. Bde transport to Wormhout	
	22.7.17		Coy Coy left by aerodrome of St Jan Der Biezen 1pm. Coy entrained at St Jan Der Biezen at 10.15pm Tilt & a mile	
	23.7.17		Coy arrived St Jan Der Biezen 2am. Coy resting	
	24.7.17		Early reconnaissance road to Canal Bank by O.C. masters & 4 masters CM G.O. of forthcoming operations	
	25.7.17		Tactical reconnaissance by O.O. 2/Lt & Z.A Sniper R.P. Building party went to Canal Bank.	
	26.7.17		Party of officers & N.C.Os reconnoitred positions in line. Coy training	
	27.7.17		Coy training	
	28.7.17		Coy moved from Z Camp to Champ Vlamertinghe Woods	
	29.7.17		Coy resting during day. Parties for wire moved into position at Canal Bank	
	30.7.17		[illegible handwritten paragraph]	
	to 31.7.17		[illegible handwritten paragraph]	

WAR DIARY

143/48 M. G. Coy.

1st Aug. 1917 — 31. Aug. 1917.

Army Form C. 2118.

WAR DIARY
or
INTELLIGENCE SUMMARY.
(Erase heading not required.)

Instructions regarding War Diaries and Intelligence Summaries are contained in F.S. Regs., Part II. and the Staff Manual respectively. Title pages will be prepared in manuscript.

Place	Date	Hour	Summary of Events and Information	Remarks and references to Appendices
Vlamertinghe	1.8.17		Coy resting in VLAMERTINGHE Woods. Heavy rain	
	2.8.17		Coy resting. Rain & cold day	
	3.8.17		Coy resting	
	4.8.17		Coy resting. 2/Lt HEATON went on leave to UK	
	5.8.17		D Section under 2/Lt MAY went into the line with 4 guns, under command of 1/5th A.&S.H.	
	6.8.17		2/Lt MAY and 1 O.R. killed by shell fire. 2/Lt HAYES took over command of guns in the line	
	7.8.17		2/Lt MAY buried in cemetery at VLAMERTINGHE	
	8.8.17		2/Lt JAMES and 6 section relieve 2/Lt HAYES and D section in the line	
	9.8.17		One section in the line. Swing in nights at four emplacements	
	10.8.17		1 O.R. killed and 16 O.Rs gassed	
	11.8.17		2/Lt SPINK and a section relieves 2/Lt JAMES and 6 section in the line	
	12.8.17		Ruts to S.A.A. dump recommended by 2/Lt NORRIS at night. 2/Lt NORRIS & party of 30 men carrier SAA from OXLONG farm to altered farm.	
	13.8.17		Party of 70 O.R's under 2/Lts James & 2/Lt Hayes carried SAA to altered. 2/Lt NORRIS + 78 section relieved 6 section in the line. 2/Lt SPINK to behind period and went back to REIGERSBERG CAMP. A dangerous scheme for attack in 16th inst on the enemy trench front & altered front. Sheet 7 100,000 maps. 70 next between 24 guns + 3 Hayes took enemy front & altered.	
	14-8-17		32 field were emplaced to altered + any in & were laid for barrage with guns in support. 7 attack to round to altered.	
	15.8.17		145 2/Lt Bell in temperature hut D20 + 4 (ref Trench SHEET 1/10,000) were heavily shelled. Artillery continued the shelling of our trenches	
	16.8.17		145 Coy Lt attacked at dawn; attack failed as one by four 3 barrages in support the attack. 20,000 rounds fired & were issued.	

Army Form C. 2118.

WAR DIARY
or
INTELLIGENCE SUMMARY.
(Erase heading not required.)

Instructions regarding War Diaries and Intelligence Summaries are contained in F. S. Regs., Part II. and the Staff Manual respectively. Title pages will be prepared in manuscript.

Place	Date	Hour	Summary of Events and Information	Remarks and references to Appendices
	16th		[illegible handwritten entry]	
	17th			
	18th			
	19th			
	20th / 21st			
	22			
	23/24			
	25			
	26			
	27th			

Army Form C. 2118.

WAR DIARY
or
INTELLIGENCE SUMMARY.
(Erase heading not required.)

Instructions regarding War Diaries and Intelligence Summaries are contained in F. S. Regs., Part II. and the Staff Manual respectively. Title pages will be prepared in manuscript.

Place	Date	Hour	Summary of Events and Information	Remarks and references to Appendices
	28th 29th		Two men withdrawn to Regimental Camp. Two remain retain relieved in due to ill health by 2 Soldiers at Regimental	
	30th		moved to Mpanga Coy went to camp at 8.9pm to Rieza	
	31		Coy proc. camp. Claimed to whether Refreshme	

Robt Joseph Kerr
Captain, 143rd ?. S. Coy.

WAR DIARY

143 MACHINE GUN COY.

1st ~~AUG~~ SEPT. 1917 — 30th SEPT. 1917.

Army Form C. 2118.

WAR DIARY
or
INTELLIGENCE SUMMARY.
(Erase heading not required.)

Instructions regarding War Diaries and Intelligence Summaries are contained in F. S. Regs., Part II. and the Staff Manual respectively. Title pages will be prepared in manuscript.

Place	Date	Hour	Summary of Events and Information	Remarks and references to Appendices
In the Field	1/9/17		Company resting at Devonshire Camp.	
	2/9/17	11 am.	Brigade Church Service 11 am.	
	3/9/17		Capt J. Willcox proceeded to Boulogne on leave.	
	4/9/17		German aeroplanes active at night.	
	5/9/17		2nd Lt Whyte proceeded to for 3 days Lg Course	
	6/9/17			
	7/9/17		2nd Lt Whyte returned from Lg Course. Lt Norris returned from leave.	
	8/9/17		2nd Lt Blake proceeded to England on leave.	
	9/9/17	11 am.	Brigade Church Service.	
	10/9/17	9-20 pm	One M.G. (A.A) fired on German plane	
	11/9/17		2nd Lt D'Azeree won 3 days P.L. Course in Camp.	
	12.9.17		Coy training at TUNNELLING CAMP.	
	13.9.17		Firing on range	
	14.9.17		3 ORs proceeded to sixth Army Rest Camp. Lt Norris proceeded on A.A. course with G.R. Arty	
	15.9.17		Bde Church Parade	
	16.9.17		Coy ran system of transport entrances at ABEELE & proceeded to AUDRUICQ O. was detaining	
	17.9.17		Coy marched to AUTINGUES	
			Bde Tactical Scheme	
	19.9.17		Coy inspection. Advanced Gun drill	
	20.9.17		Scheme "A" fired on Guery range	
	21.9.17		Advanced Gun drill & Fire Control	
	22.9.17			
	23.9.17		Church Parade attached with 1/6 R.War.R	
	24.9.17		Bde Tactical Scheme	
	25.9.17		Bde Tactical Scheme	

Army Form C. 2118.

WAR DIARY
or
INTELLIGENCE SUMMARY.
(Erase heading not required.)

Place	Date	Hour	Summary of Events and Information	Remarks and references to Appendices
	26.9.17		Batt tactical Scheme	
	27.9.17		Coy Interior	
	28.9.17		Batt tactical Scheme	
	29.9.17		Preparing for move	
	30.9.17		Coy moved by tram to DAMBRE CAMP	

A. W. Joseph Lieut.
O.C. "C" Coy. 143rd M. G. Coy.

WAR DIARY.

143RD MACHINE GUN COMPANY

1st Oct. 1917 —

31st Oct. 1917.

Army Form C. 2118.

WAR DIARY
or
INTELLIGENCE SUMMARY.
(Erase heading not required.)

Instructions regarding War Diaries and Intelligence Summaries are contained in F. S. Regs., Part II. and the Staff Manual respectively. Title pages will be prepared in manuscript.

Place	Date	Hour	Summary of Events and Information	Remarks and references to Appendices
DAMORE CAMP VLAMERTINGHE	Oct 1 1917	10.0am	Company billeted in Tents.	
			Half a dozen A.V. shells fell round about the camp. None in it	
		evening	Enemy aeroplanes dropped bombs. Horse dropped in camp	
	2nd	7am	Enemy plane dropped bombs in camp. Cpl DENNE slightly wounded	
		12noon	Officers and section leaders go up the line in to buss reconnoitring.	
		3.0pm	Company buses to REIGERSBURG CAMP	
	3rd	evening	Final arrangements made before going into the line	
		5.0pm	Company buses up into Assembly Position	
In the line	4th	6am	Attack just ordered to go over unsupportedinformation as units	
		2pm	2 guns under 2nd Lt Hayward to TWEED HOUSE (D Section)	
		2pm	2 guns under 2nd Lt BROWN at WINCHESTER FARM (D Section) } under Lt DE JONGH
		2pm	commanded by Lt TURNER to WINCHESTER FARM (A Section)	
		2pm	under Lieut Norris to go to C BURNS HOUSE in 2nd Phase (B Section)	
		2pm	2nd Lt WHYTE to ALBATROSS FARM (A Section) C Section in reserve at HUBNER FARM	
		2pm	under 2nd Lt CHARLESLEY to WELLINGTON (B Section) Company HQ. also	
			Situation as under TWEED HOUSE under 2nd Lt HAYWARD	
		8.0am	2 guns (D Section + B Section)	
		2 guns	(2 sections extension) at ALBATROSS FARM under 2nd Lt Whyte	
		1 gun	(B section) in front of WINCHESTER (a Wellington) under Lt Holyfield	
		10am	Lieut Shaffrey brought two platoons of C section to reinforce WINCHESTER	
		11.9pm	Lieut Shaffrey & 3 others came up to YORK HOUSE ready to push on with infantry at 6pm The attack failed and Lieut Shaffrey's four were driven back from the late new position to the left of WINCHESTER and 2 guns to WELLINGTON Total advance during the day 200 yards.	

A7092). Wt. W1289/M1291 750,000. 1/17. D. D & L, Ltd. Forms/C2118/14.

Army Form C. 2118.

WAR DIARY
or
INTELLIGENCE SUMMARY.
(Erase heading not required.)

Instructions regarding War Diaries and Intelligence Summaries are contained in F.S. Regs., Part II. and the Staff Manual respectively. Title pages will be prepared in manuscript.

Place	Date	Hour	Summary of Events and Information	Remarks and references to Appendices
ST JULIEN.	Oct. 5		Company remains in their position. Intermittent shelling.	
	6		do	
	7	9pm	Company relieved by 145 M.G. Coy never been to IRISH FARM	
	8	2pm	Company moves to M.G.C. Camp by lorry.	
POPERINGHE	9	10 am	March billets in POPERINGHE. Lt HAMPSON + 2nd Lt HALE join the Company	
			Total Casualties during last spell of fighting	
			2nd Lieut PETURNER Returning to Duty	Killed Wounded Missing Died from Wounds & Missing
			Lieut G NORRIS. wounded	O.Rs.
			2nd Lt E. BROWN wounded	6 21 4 3 1
			" G.W. MAYWARD wounded	
	10	–	Cleaning arms and reorganising Company.	
	11	–	do 2nd Lt Bafon Jones joins the Company.	
	12	–	do	
	13	7pm	Entrain at PEZELHOEK	
MONT ST ELOI	14	10 am	Detrain at MAROEUIL and march to MONT ST ELOI.	
		3.10pm	Capt Willett goes up reconnoitring	
VIMY.	15	50pm	March up line to relieve 4th Canadian Machine Gun Company	
			Very quiet	
	16	10am	Enemy raid 31st Division on our right. Enemy puts gas shells near to batteries	
	17		Very quiet	
			do	

Army Form C. 2118.

WAR DIARY
or
INTELLIGENCE SUMMARY.
(Erase heading not required.)

Instructions regarding War Diaries and Intelligence Summaries are contained in F. S. Regs., Part II. and the Staff Manual respectively. Title pages will be prepared in manuscript.

Place	Date	Hour	Summary of Events and Information	Remarks and references to Appendices
VIMY	18—28		Very quiet nothing to report Pte Taylor wounded	
	28.		Very quiet and nothing to report.	
	29		do	
	30		do	
	31	6pm	Relieved by 145M & Company go back to normand Transport lines at AUX RIETZ.	

Ashleyph Lieut

www.ingramcontent.com/pod-product-compliance
Lightning Source LLC
Chambersburg PA
CBHW081549160426
43191CB00011B/1878